# Another Wet Saturday

## Village Verses and Views

by

## Colin Gates

**Another Wet Saturday: Village Verses and Views**

First published in the UK in 2021 by Stanford Publishing

Copyright © 2021 Stanford Publishing Limited

ISBN 978-1-999-35553-1

The right of Colin Gates to be identified as the author has been asserted by him in accordance with the Copyright, Designs and Patents Act, 1988.

British Library Cataloguing in Publication Data. A catalogue record for this book is available from the British Library.

Typeset in Minion Pro and Century Gothic
by 2m Partnership Limited  www.2m.org.uk

Printed and bound in the UK by Book Empire, Leeds

Stanford Publishing Limited
24 Chapel Road
Stanford in the Vale
Faringdon
Oxfordshire
SN7 8LE
UK
Tel: +44(0)1367 710677

Email: enquiries@stanfordpublishing.co.uk

Website: www.stanfordpublishing.co.uk

# Contents

# Foreword
by
## Martyn Wyndham-Read

Since his early days, Colin Gates has been very aware of the traditions of the countryside and of its songs handed down through the ages which are so important for the culture of our country. This enthusiasm has been transfered to Colin's poems, illustrations and writings.

With his poems being imposed on such solid foundations, some of them have become songs themselves for all of us and future generations to enjoy. Colin's knowledge of Charlwood village is deep-rooted, passionate and well-recorded musically and in literature.

I am delighted to have been well acquainted with Colin since our musical beginnings as *The Black Diamonds* - an eager and aspiring local skiffle group formed in the late 1950's.

I have had the pleasure to continue to be closely associated with Colin at many musical events in Charlwood and beyond. I have also much enjoyed the well-deserved success of his latest book *Tales From Beyond The Old Parish Pump*, glimpsing into Charlwood's history.

This collection of his poems and drawings continues Colin's literary accomplishments.

*The bygone years are fading fast*
*And dimly they are seen.*
*Yet old songs glowing in the past*
*Illuminate the dream.*
*Listen to the old song,*
*Its story and its tune*
*For looking back, it lights the track*
*From the sunrise to the moon.*

Colin Gates

## Introduction and a note about the Notes

During the dark days of the covid virus-induced lockdowns of 2020, like many fellow prisoners, I thought it might be a good idea to busy myself at home. I made the mistake of starting off shredding old and out-of-date paperwork but got no further than a box-file full of scraps of paper on which were various verses I had written over the years, some of them dating back to the mid 1960's.

Other boxes and binders in the loft and the study revealed more of the same, among them songs I had written and performed, or intended to perform, with the folk groups Arky's Toast and One Knight Only. During this period of search, find and collate we also found a number of pencil sketches, also dating back many years. We filed the sketches with the verse and noticed that certain sketches seemed to sit well alongside certain poems. The idea of a book was born.

Pages 127 to 143 contain notes about some of the poems and a brief explanation of the event, person or circumstances which prompted me to put pen to the many scraps of paper.

Special thanks are due to my wife Susie for her never-ending patience, encouragement, suggestions and for helping me to tidy the study; which we never finished. Also, I would like to thank Ian Agnew for again giving so much time and encouragement to one of my projects and for liaising with Richard Astell of Stanford Publishing who, along with his excellent team, brought this project to life. Thanks are also due to Ian's wife Mandy for agreeing to be 'the man in the street' and acting as a 'sounding board' when she read through the draft of the book.

Finally, a big thank you to Martyn Wyndham-Read for his kind comments in the Foreword and for including some of my songs, which are in this book, in his repertoire.

I stood in Black Ditch in the drizzle and the gloom of a January Saturday when eleven men in blue shirts emerged from the old Half Moon's back-yard and ran along the footpath toward the football pitch. It was 1950 and the football team were using the pub as their changing room for home matches. As they ran, their hard leather studs crunched and clattered on the surface of the ancient stone path.

"Up the Blues!" I shouted, but with little enthusiasm as the rainwater dripped down the back of my neck and seeped into the soles of my shoes. Two hours later, defeated and deflated the team crunched back again, heads down and at a much slower pace. It was still raining.

"Up the Blues!" I shouted, but with even less enthusiasm.

# Another Wet Saturday

The tramp and the trudge of the blue clad men
Rings clear on a winter's day
Out in the Half Moon yard and then
Over the causes slate grey.
Out through the drizzle and darkening hues
To the cry 'Up the blues, up the blues.'

The old yard door swings back with a thud
On another wet Saturday
And Black Ditch echoes to many a stud
As they crunch where the grey stone lay.
Out in the rain to win or to lose
As we shout 'Up the blues, up the blues!'

But they can't find the goal that they seek
After ninety minutes or more.
'But things will be different next week'
Says one of the spectators four
As gravely he bears the sad news
Of defeat and the rout of the blues.

Both weary and wet the blue clad men
Tramp back in the gathering gloom.
In through the old yard door again
To the bar and the little back room.
But soon the beer and strong cider they choose
Will cheer up the blues. 'Up the blues.'

# A Chat with Sir John

We talked about the artist's fame
That day there in the hall
A portrait in a gilded frame
That lent against the wall
But I wanted to talk of the Aldershot sun
And a lady he called Miss Joan Hunter Dunn

He mentioned the transition
Of shadow to light
And the clever composition
Of the Lady in White
He pointed to brush strokes and texture and tone
But said not a word of the lady he'd known.

I wanted to ask him
Of what he thought now
Of Westbury-on-Trym
Or of Henley and Slough
But perspective and colour were so much more fun
And no mention was made of Miss Joan Hunter Dunn.

The urgent ring of the telephone bell
Very soon made him aware
That the lady was able to see him now
And the elevator dinged by the stair
As he went to the room where her ladyship dwells
I thought it quite apt he'd been summoned by bells.

## Where Purple Orchis Grew

An old woman told me once,
As she talked about her childhood,
How she walked the hills and valleys
And rambled through the wildwood.
    'It was on Stan Hill,' she said,
    'And onward far beyond
    Through the sleeping village
    Then through the farm and on.'

    'We passed the yellow daffodils
    And white violets growing wild.
    On to where the mushrooms grew
    And the golden stooks were piled.
    We knew the different grasses
    Out where the wild geese flew
    Over lovely little cowslips
    Where purple orchis grew.'

## The Fields Lie Silent Now

The sky is high and wide tonight
Above the silent mill,
The last rays of the winter sun
Lay gold upon the hill.
Then from the shadow of the wood
I hear the first owl's cry
And silver pools left by the plough
Hold the first star in the sky.

Gone the leaf and gone the lark
The wild rose and the plough
The birds have flown their summer home
The fields lie silent now.

Dark furrows climbing Great High Field
Guide the crow back to his nest
Where the oaks stand interlaced
Against the golden west.
Frost creeps in upon the land
With deep December cold.
All the fields lie silent now
The year is growing old.

Gone the leaf and gone the lark
The wild rose and the plough
The birds have flown their summer home
The fields lie silent now.

Red berries in the bare hedgerow
And acorns on the ground
Fade slowly in the dying light
As darkness folds around.
The fields and woods together now
Their winter secrets keep
With the beauty of the autumn
Just a dream recalled in sleep.

Gone the leaf and gone the lark
The wild rose and the plough
The birds have flown their summer home
The fields lie silent now.

The sky is high, the sky is wide
Above the silent mill
And Mother nature sleeps tonight
On the dark side of the hill
But as the seasons slowly turn
And when the sky is blue
The buds of May will tell the tale
Of her power to renew.

Gone the leaf and gone the lark
The wild rose and the plough
The birds have flown their summer home
The fields lie silent now.

# The 95th Came Home Today

The 95th came home today
In their jackets green
With fife and drum along the way
So glorious to be seen.
They formed up by the Guard Room door
From whence they marched in times before.

Returning through the centuries
From the field of Waterloo
To the chapel by the trees
And the Guard Room they once knew.
The Rifles in the muddy lane
Report for duty once again.

Standing guard, they told the story
Of battles in old Boney's war
Tales of valour and of glory
And the death of brave John Moore.
When Marshal Soult was swept aside
On the day his army died.

On the ridge at Waterloo
In the misty morning light
They made The Duke a warming brew
To prepare him for the coming fight.
At the Chapel door they say
The 95th came home today.

## The Ghost of Betty Neighbour

There was a chill in the gloom of the little back room.
Even the candle flame shivered
To the haunting air of the old singer there
As the last notes faded and quivered.
His song told the story of valour and glory,
As we sat by the guttering glow,
Of the battle that day out there in the bay.
When they carried his Lordship below.

The song of the fight drifted into the night,
As clear as a ship's ringing bell,
To a place by the wood where a hovel once stood
And old Betty Neighbour did dwell.
Her spirit was stirred by familiar word.
She had sung the same song long ago.
And told the same story of valour and glory
When they carried Lord Nelson below.

There was a chill in the gloom of the little back room
When Betty joined in with the song.
She was eager to tell of how Nelson fell
And how he was carried along.
Of her presence there none were aware
As they shivered all in a row.
She told them the tale, how beneath Victory's sail
Her father bore Nelson below.

# They Sang the Barrel Dry

When the men of Tanyards drank their fill,
On harvest supper day,
The autumn wind from off the hill
Bore the songs away.
They joined old voices in the air
From harvest days gone by.
When other feet walked out to meet
And sing the barrel dry.

Lost voices sing in harmony
As autumn breezes blow.
Singing their old songs to me
The songs of long ago.
I feel their lives move closer now
Beneath the harvest sky.
Borne by the sound of chorus round
When they sang the barrel dry.

The last half load is on the ground.
The sun is sinking low
There's time to have another round
And a song before we go.
Many a tale has been told
Of harvest days gone by
When they tossed the pot and drank the lot
And sang the barrel dry.

Old harvest nights are fading fast
Into the distant time
But lanterns glowing in the past
Upon the singers shine.
As I listen to the old song
They raise their voices high.
I see the men who gathered when
They drank the barrel dry.

## Missing from the Choir

How sad they are, the men who ring
A quarter peal of Old Grandsire
Yet still they join the rest to sing
Along with ladies of the choir.

They sing an ancient country song
The Red Rose and the Briar.
They sing it well; they sing it strong
But one is missing from the choir.

For her they sing The Last Farewell
Their voices rising higher.
It was for her they rang the passing bell
For she is missing from the choir.

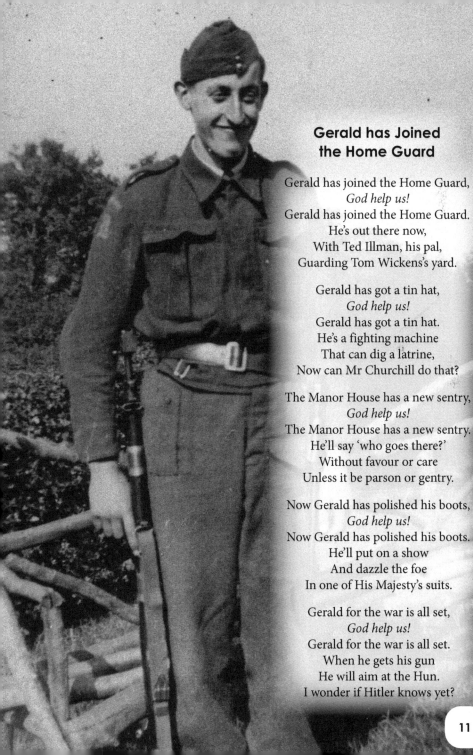

## Gerald has Joined the Home Guard

Gerald has joined the Home Guard,
*God help us!*
Gerald has joined the Home Guard.
He's out there now,
With Ted Illman, his pal,
Guarding Tom Wickens's yard.

Gerald has got a tin hat,
*God help us!*
Gerald has got a tin hat.
He's a fighting machine
That can dig a latrine,
Now can Mr Churchill do that?

The Manor House has a new sentry,
*God help us!*
The Manor House has a new sentry.
He'll say 'who goes there?'
Without favour or care
Unless it be parson or gentry.

Now Gerald has polished his boots,
*God help us!*
Now Gerald has polished his boots.
He'll put on a show
And dazzle the foe
In one of His Majesty's suits.

Gerald for the war is all set,
*God help us!*
Gerald for the war is all set.
When he gets his gun
He will aim at the Hun.
I wonder if Hitler knows yet?

11

# The Women in Red
## (AD 851)

The Northern Men came off the hill
Beneath the Raven Banner.
They came to plunder and to kill
And burn down Hall and Manor.
Thunder rolled down Aclea Crest
When village men went forth
To join the ceorls from Saxon west
And meet the savage of the north.

Echoing through the darkened Weald,
For years and years, the old folk said,
Came haunting sound of axe on shield
And hillside water flowing red.
As sun went down, from out the woods
There came a Viking band
Waylaid by women in red hoods,
Shining blades in hand.

Some men died there on the ridge
At Rawbones, where they turned and fled.
The last man died at Killmans Bridge
Where waited women dressed in red.
The blood has gone from High Barebones.
Only legend now remains
How in defence of hearth and homes
They brought Valhalla to the Danes.

# A Winter Walk

The pale-yellow orb of the watery sun
Silhouettes the bare branches
Where winter has come
To the banks of the stream
Where ice-locked and sealed
The roots of the willow once stood revealed.

Like hawthorn the cold air claws at my face
But I turn up my collar
And quicken my pace.
Through bracken where dry leaves
And grey winter grass
Shake in the east wind and sigh as I pass.

Mud ruts and ice pools crunch under my shoe
As I walk by the field side
Where the summer corn grew
And the path through the wood
Leads powdered with snow
To the pale-yellow wash of the sun sinking low.

## Eighty Years Ago, Today

Eighty years ago, today
I entered from stage right
To stroll my hour upon the boards
Briefly in the bright spot-light.
For a while the foot-lights glow
On my small part here, in the show.

The old man waved his paper high
'Peace in our time' he proudly quipped
'No more fighting, no more war.'
But Hitler had not read the script.
Across the world the stage lights dimmed,
The sounds of war borne on the wind.

And I first saw the light of day
With black-out curtains down.
The fierce fight raging in the skies
Above the village and the town.
Into the battle I was born
As lights were lowered in the storm.

Eighty years ago, today
Fire burned and people died
And in the darkness of the hour
A new born baby woke and cried.
Since that day a bonus true
Is each day's light that shines a' new.

# An Ancient Path in Modern Times

I walked my dog down by the stream
That runs beside Great Steven's Crawl
And where the old crack willows lean
I heard the blackbird's fluted call
Then saw the minnows in the flow
On a hidden bend where dark reeds grow.

Suddenly, with back-thrust scream,
A giant liner, losing height,
Shattered the peaceful summer scene
As it sought the final landing light.
The blackbird ceased melodious rhymes
And I cursed the progress of the times.

Crackling static filled the air
After the monster had passed on by
But sun shone on the river where
A brilliant flash had caught my eye
The Kingfisher's red and turquoise flame
Raised my spirits once again.

An ancient path in modern times
Took me down once peaceful ways
Where landing lights now stand in lines
And take off slots divide the days.
Though metal monsters fill the sky
The 'fisher still delights the eye.

# Darkness in the Evergreen

In all the seasons of the plough
The dancing children there had seen
The autumn berries on the bough
And darkness in the evergreen.
For a thousand years they came and played
Around the trunk on harvest morn
Before they knelt in church and prayed
In thanks for wheat and golden corn.

The wind will blow and the fire may burn
But still I watch the seasons turn.
In autumn weathers fair or foul
You'll see the berries on the bough.

In dark December's stormy blast
He pondered where the branches bend
'Will my children be the last
To dance around this ancient friend?'
'When in the Wyld,' the old tree sighed,
'Through distant years and long-lost time
We grew together side by side
And your roots run deep like mine.'

The wind will blow and the fire may burn
But still I watch the seasons turn.
In autumn weathers fair or foul
You'll see the berries on the bough.

'As sure as rain falls from the sky
For many long years I know I'll see
Your children's children dancing by
Beneath my coal black canopy.
In all the harvest times 'til now
Down where the branches twist and lean
They saw the berries on the bough
And darkness in the evergreen.'

## If the Stones Could Only Speak

If the stones could only speak
What a story they would tell
Of each and every parish man
From birth to passing bell.
For a thousand years they gathered
And knelt beside the wall.
The rich man and the poor man
The wise man and the fool.

The men came back from Senlac
To haul and cut the stone.
The walls they made remain today
And were built on Saxon bone.
They tell of serf and suffering
Beneath the Norman banner
And monks sent off a wandering
When John stole back the manor.

Two centuries passed on as a day
And Crusaders were returning
To build an aisle to the south
As the Holy Land lay burning.
Then an artist put the fear of God
Into Mass on Sunday morning
By painting on the new laid stones,
Death and gospel warning.

If the stones could only speak
And tell to us the story,
The tears of generations gone
And moments of brief glory.
The pain and persecution
And then the sabres rattle
When masons passed this way again
And built the Chantry Chapel.

Today I stood by the old north wall
As the masons come and go
And heard the old stones tell the new
Of everything they know.
The war and greed and poverty
Remain until this day
And if the stones could only speak
Would we turn our heads away?

## The Echo of the Big Trombone

Parson Gibson began to moan
And then he swore and cursed
When tuba, drum and big trombone
Of the village band rehearsed.
Around the pond and down the lawn
The band went marching by.
When Jarvie played his silver horn
Alleluia filled the sky.

Cows and sheep were on the run
As the peace was shattered.
When Samuel beat the big bass drum
The hens and geese were scattered.
In and out and round about
Went the big trombone
Which made the Parson rave and shout
Hellfire and Brimstone!

They stood defiant and no one spoke,
As the air turned blue,
And then, at last, the nerve was broke
Of Samuel and his crew.
They turned around and ran for home
Led by the silver horn
But tuba, drum and big trombone
Lay scattered on the lawn.

No more we'll hear the tuba play
Nor Samuel beat the drum
For brass and woodwind on that day
Were sent to kingdom come
But late at night you'll hear a moan
Down by the old church tower
And the echo of a big trombone
When midnight strikes the hour.

They played the good old Harvest Home,
A Tango and a Rumba
But the echo of the big trombone
Disturbed the Parson's slumber.

21

# Keep in b' the Wall

'Keep in b' the wall as you go on your way'.
'Keep in b' the wall.' We heard him say.

For the south-west wind
And its cohort the rain.
Tear through the blackthorn
And roar up the lane.

Keep in b' the wall as the cold winds moan.
Keep in b' the wall, it will guide your way home.

We'd drunk the whiskey
By his fireside bright
And his sad old songs
Near lasted the night.

Keep in b' the wall the south-westerly roared.
Keep in b' the wall. Who knows what's abroad?

We'd heard the old tales
And told some of our own.
Now the cold, early dawn
Will light our way home.

So, we'll keep in b' the wall as we walk in the rain.
Keep in b' the wall 'till we meet him again.

## The Corner of the Field

I love to see the great high oak
Where black crow circles high above
And furrows stretching far away
But another thing I love
Are little hidden corners
Where hedge meets woodland ride
And rusty hinge and gatepost
And twisted tree trunk hide.

I hear the poplars whisper
To a blushing pastel sky
And dark reeds growing from the bank
Are pleasing to my eye
But, there, beneath the brambles
Where the footpath turns away
A silent pool lies hidden
And reflects the close of day.

The new moon hangs above the wood
And as I walk along the lane
I see the last rays of the sun
Set autumn leaves aflame.
Yet amid the beauty all around
I love the view concealed
Of mossy bank and broken fence
Behind the corner of the field.

# Don't go by Way of the Old Church Walk

Don't go by way of the Old Church Walk
On dark nights such as these.
Deep shadows through the graveyard stalk
And linger 'neath the trees.
It's best go round by Rectory Lane
Where windows lend their light.
Endure for longer in the rain
Than meet a spectral sight.

All those names of childhood
Gathered there beneath the tower
Must still be friendly, kind and good
Despite the darkness and the hour.
But there's one of which I was not fond,
She lies in wait there for a sign
That I have lingered by her pond
With my rod and knotted line.

A fearsome soul who counted newts
And chastised me both loud and long
For wearing of my wellington boots
At Sunday service evensong.
On second thoughts perhaps you're right
She may be waiting there again
And I'm without a tie on Sunday night.
I think we'll go by Rectory Lane!

## Farewell to the Fields

I walked once more that leafy lane
To see the Rainbow Woods again
Where, as boys, we chased our dreams
Across the fields and winding streams.
Around Floods Hole and up the hill
To Greenings then to Puckney Ghyll
And every field and wood below
Had names they knew so long ago.

From Skewers Mead to Pickle Hall
We saw the kestrel turn and fall
Then chased the deer the many miles
From Loggerhead across High Stiles.
Then on Mount Noddy far away
Where the evening shadows lay
Too far to hear the church bells ring
We heard the dappled night bird sing.

As sun went down, we played our game
In Steven's Crawl and Pudding Lane,
Until, with moon on leaf and thorn,
We wandered home through silver corn,
But years have gone and men now try
To raze the trees and fill the sky
And take away those fields of home
Where as a boy I used to roam.

As I walked out in the fields again
I thought of men who'd loved them when
There was no mighty engines roar
Where their fathers walked before.
Their father's, fathers ploughed the ground
To nothing but the sweet birds sound
And called each field by its olden name
Will all their love now be in vain?

Farewell to the fields
And the peace that they bring
There's a mighty roar waiting
Where the sweet song birds sing.

## As we Followed Billy Poole

From Pudding Croft to Ladylands
We searched for Billy Poole
Then from the gloom of Telvet Copse
We heard the clarion call.
Old Red was in the Denchure Field
And red was in the sky
As for the Fatting Hovel
We too were in full cry.

Then came the bay of Southern Hound
When Billy cracked his whip
But in the early morning mist
Old Red gave him the slip.
Way back along the Denchure Field
With never sight nor sound
And we raced off to Ladylands
Behind old Billy's hound.

Across Bakeworth the school bell rang
Its daily morning chime
But greeted by the silent lane
It rang a second time.
We heard the hound. We heard the hoof
And Billy's hunting horn
But school was distanced far behind
That red November morn.

For Billy's call had stirred our blood
Beyond all guilt and sorrow
And in the chase, we little feared
The trouble of the morrow.
When Fatting Hovel came in sight
We still were in full cry
For Red was in the field that day
And red was in our eye.

We ran the length of Rainbow Wood
And skirted Pickle Hall
With the devil in our stride that day
As we followed Billy Poole.

## From the Old Half Moon to the Rising Sun

In summer time beneath the sun
When larks are singing sweet
We'll work our best 'till day is done
Then old friends we will greet.
Let's hope that we shall meet again
And drink in social glasses
And our toast be to Charlwood's men
And Charlwood's bonny lasses.

And so, we'll walk that dusty road
That's the longest in the land.
From the old Half Moon
to the Rising Sun
With our pint pots in our hand.

When soon or late we reach that coast
O'er life's rough ocean driven
May we rejoice no wanderers lost
A family in heaven.
Give us strong drink until we blink
When sinking in despair
And liquor good to fire our blood
When depressed with grief and care.

And so, we'll walk that dusty road
That's the longest in the land.
From the old Half Moon
to the Rising Sun
With our pint pots in our hand.

So, let us booze and deep carouse
With bumpers flowing o'er
Till we forget our loves and debts
And mind our griefs no more.
Then sit around when shearing's done
And drinking strong ale brown
With the Half Moon rising in the sky
And the red sun going down.

And so, we'll walk that dusty road
That's the longest in the land.
From the old Half Moon
to the Rising Sun
With our pint pots in our hand.

## Parson's Field

Dying embers in the orchard dew
As in the charcoal days of old
Send thin smoke up into the blue
And gathering crystal cold.
Flying in the west skies white
And transparent glow of red
The last crow sees the hand of night
Enfold a day now cold and dead.

Walking in the autumn weald
The Saxon as he sowed
Ordained the shape of Parson's Field
And the wandering village road
And flowing there a silver stream
Once passed beneath the bough
But homeward crow is seldom seen
Amid the concrete now.

Tarmac strips lie on the land
Where once the ploughman stood
To guide his team with steady hand
At the edge of Brockley Wood
The wandering ways the Saxon came
Now skirt the neon light
And for Parson's Field I search in vain
This still November night.

# A Thousand Bells Will Ring Tonight

A thousand bells will ring tonight
To wish the old goodbye.
A thousand beacons shine their light
Into the winter sky.
The chimes of celebrations rise
Above the old church tower
And a thousand years will fade away
When midnight strikes the hour.

Only yesterday, it seems, by chance
We began to dream
Of where the seven sisters dance
Beside the silver stream.
Now we set out tomorrow,
Before the morning sun,
As hands reach out there for the stars
On a journey just begun.

A thousand stars yet out of sight
Await our hopes and fears
And the bells ring a farewell tonight
To the ghosts of former years.
As we move out from shadows deep
Into the morning glow
A star-ship will be waiting
Across the void to go.

On chapters of deep sorrow
The ringers turn the page
But waiting still tomorrow
Will be the hatred and the rage.
Too many shadows linger
As the morning bell is rung
And the same old ghosts still haunt us now
As when the world was young.

# The Old Songs

From the rising sun to the pale moon
Slowly turns the day.
From morning dew through heat of noon
Till darkness shrouds the way.
Hear their ancient story
That continues to unfold.
From springs fresh green and summer scene
To autumns burning gold.

The bygone years are fading fast
And dimly they are seen.
Yet old songs glowing in the past
Illuminate the dream.
Listen to the old song,
Its story and its tune
For looking back, it lights the track
From the sunrise to the moon.

# The Rusty Old Tin Helmet

In Jarvie Ellis's garden at the edge of Dandies Meadow
There's violet and forget-me-not and daises white and yellow
But there among the cabbage on a wooden pole you'll see
A rusty old tin helmet of the village L.D.V.

Now when they called for volunteers to guard the summer sky
He put the old tin helmet on and kissed his wife goodbye.
Up and down the lane they marched 'till it was nearly noon
And then to proudly guard the beer inside the old Half Moon.

They marched along together with Samuel from the band
And old Tom Franks not far behind with pitchfork in his hand.
But Jarvie wore the helmet for all the world to see
That rusty old tin helmet of the village L.D.V.

But that was forty years ago and when the war was done
He sat down by the apple tree and put aside his gun.
That rusty old tin helmet stayed there in wind and rain
Waiting for the time old Jarvie marched again.

Now westward you may hear Drake's drum when danger threatens near
But in the garden late at night it's Jarvie's steps you'll hear
Marching down with old Tom Franks and Samuel from the band
In a rusty old tin helmet of the L.D.V. so grand.

They marched along together with Samuel from the band
And old Tom Franks not far behind with pitchfork in his hand
But Jarvie wore the helmet for all the world to see
That rusty old tin helmet of the village L.D.V.

# A Landscape Ever New

He couldn't paint the southern wind
A' racing on its way
Over endless fields of stubbled gold
That late September day.
Its journeys through the tall grass
His eager eye would fill.
As it hurried to its vanishing point
On the blue and distant hill.

He couldn't draw the crackling sound
Of the barley's line and form
As bearded heads go whispering
To the young and dancing corn.
He saw a wash of peacefulness,
An exercise in shade,
As night creeps in upon the land
At daylight's gentle fade.

He couldn't sketch the scent of rose
As it hangs above the nettle
Where wild hawthorn holds the moon
And painted ladies settle.
The smell of wood-smoke in the lane
And the vixen's startled call
Were the memories of summer
He could not paint at all.

He could only stand in wonder
When the mist and autumn dew
And the scented sounds of summer
Made a landscape ever new.

# God Save our Squire

Here's to this place and the people that's here
Sitting and supping all drinking good beer.
Now spare a thought for those gone before
Who sat in this house both rich and both poor.
An old man once told me of the folk he once knew
So have one more jug while I sing to you.


There was an old man went a begging one day.
He went to the big house and this he did say,
'It's many long weeks since I had food last
If I don't eat today, I shall have to eat grass.'
The fine lady looked at his old head so bare,
'Please go 'round the back, the lawn's much longer there.'


Old Shakey had a haircut. It was a big job.
After three hours the barber did sob,
'You've caused me such heartache, sweating and toil.
Now have something on it. I can recommend oil.'
'I'll have something on it but I'll have none of that.
The only thing I want is my bloody hat!'


Now Aubrey at the football he cut a fine style.
One day on the green he made everyone smile.
The policeman in goal had let in twenty-five
But late in the game he made a fine dive
Because as he stooped to pull up his socks
Old Aubrey kicked him in the penalty box.

Now old George's wife she talked night and day.
She nagged and she nagged 'till he passed away.
The Doctor looked at him and said he was dead
But George hearing this sat up in his bed.
'Oh, I'm not gone yet. I just need a rest.'
She said, 'Hold your tongue George. The Doctor knows best!'

God save our squire and all his relations
Don't let us rise up above our own stations
And help our vicar because he is drunk
It's a gallon and a quart of good cider he's sunk.

# Violet and Woodbine

Violet and Woodbine rang the bells
Through the grass at Hatchet and Helze
And Great High Field of Wealden clay
Heard Plain Bob Doubles April Day.
Stone Pit Field and Further Lyon
Caught the sound of Charlwood iron
As over leafy copse and mere
The bells rang loud, the bells rang clear.

Great Tory Field of Crooked Neal
And Further Brownings heard the peal
And through the trees around Telvet
To Dandies Land and further yet
To Bell Pit Ponds wherein the devil
Tipped the tenor and the treble.
With no sound sweeter and no sound finer
Rang out the bells in Plain Bob Minor.

At Great Bakeworth the sound rose higher
With a quarter peal of Old Grandsire
And College Pleasure shook the tops
Of the silver trees in Edolphs Copse.
Across Rent Rolls the changes rang
And to the fields their music sang.
From Chantersluer to Guzzleshaw
The Bells rang round and round once more.

With their Violet and Woodbine rang the bells
Through the grass at Hatchet and Helze
And Great High Field of Wealden clay
Heard Plain Bob Doubles April Day.
Stone Pit Field and Further Lyon
Caught the sound of Charlwood iron.
From Windmill Plat to Brittleware
The chimes of Charlwood filled the air.

And so, the bells rang out our days
In far off fields and woodland ways
And when old time knocks on our door
The bells will ring us home once more.

## These Days My Doorbell Seldom Rings

These days my doorbell seldom rings
As I watch my fire burn,
(But I've got my garden and my cat.
I'm grateful just for having that!)
And as the hours slowly turn
I sit and think of many things.

I think of when my son was small
And Mr Butler's good advice,
(Because of those evacuees
To pay the extra in school fees)
To send him to a place that's nice
And not that common local school.

He never made a village friend
And soon he found himself in college.
(Mr Butler said he would,
Being studious and good.)
He wisely used his new found knowledge
Avoiding teenage fad and trend.

And now he has a job abroad,
Somewhere in the middle-east.
(I heard from him one day last June
And hope to see my grandson soon.)
But I sometimes wished as years increased
The good advice I had ignored.

## Tales that Skip and Dance over Time

By Killiman's Bridge
the tall grasses sigh
And recall a long-ago dream.
Told on the banks
where the waters flowed by
At the place of the sword in the stream.
At Barebones and Rawbones they stood for a while
But were left in the field of the dead.
No more to plunder on England's fair mile
After meeting the women in red.

Then high on the hill
near Hatchet and Helze
The Parson near lost his wits
When the Devil tossed high
the new parish bells
And left behind the dark pits.
From out of the night Dog Smith hobbled by
In the guise of a ragged old beggar.
Remembering how they had answered his cry
He bestowed bread and beef there forever.

But in dark Welland's Ghyll
an hour before dawn
Legend recalls a strange sound
From deep in the thicket
an old hunting horn
And the bay of the grey Southern Hound.
Like lonely lanterns that glimmer and shine
Down dark and forgotten old ways
Tales that skip and dance over time
Guide us back through the years and the days.

# The Fiddler's Shoe

Old grey men and young ones too
Dance to the rhythm of the fiddler's shoe.
The magic bow plays jigs and reels
As dancing men kick up their heels.
They jump so high to the jangle of bells
And the clash of wood as the music swells.
Old Molly Oxford comes and goes
From his Merry fingers to his dancing toes.

Dancing men one night in May
Weave and turn to The Shepherds Hay
As Jolly Martin taps his toe
And plays a tune with his magic bow.
They jump so high in the village street
To the merry song and the tabor's beat.
Up the middle turn and through
Dancing on to the fiddler's shoe.

With heel and toe on the cobbled stone
Jolly Martin led them home
But the echo of the magic bow
Fills the air where ever I go.
Through the years until the day
I heard a fiddler start to play.
Sixteen men leapt in the air
The fiddler's shoe still tapping there.

Constant Billy and Bonny Green
Oh, dear mother what a fool I've been.
Old Molly Oxford and The Hay
The fiddler's shoe still tapped away.

# Wake up Boys and Follow Tom

They say that you can hear Tom Knapp
From many miles away
Rattling, rumbling down the lane
So early in the day.
Creaking, groaning, making sparks,
Disturbing dogs and waking larks.
Belching smoke from his big stack,
A traction man is old Tom Knapp.

We filled the boiler from the pond
And soon the fire-box glowed.
Tom checked the pressure on the gauge
And sixty pounds was showed.
The four-ply belt began to hum
As we fed the corn into the drum.
Four-bushel sacks beneath the chutes
And the corn chaff blowing around our boots.

We followed Tom to Three Pit Field
And worked there for a day
Then back again to Larkins Farm
To earn the extra pay.
With scream of steam the whistle blows
And every Lord and Lady knows
When the big black stack lights up the sky
The thresher men are passing by.

Now when the threshing is all done
And all the barns are clear
We'll follow Tom to the old Half Moon
And take a jug of beer.
And when the threshers sing, they say
The song is heard from miles away,
Rattling, rumbling down the lane
As we follow Tom Knapp home again.

So wake up boys and follow Tom
And employment we may find
For there'll always be the sacks to weigh
And the straw to bind.

# That Summer on The Somme

The sun beat down on yellow grass
When he was just sixteen
And walking proudly to the crease
Out on the village green
But other team-mates waited
As the shadows crept along
To play a different sort of game
That summer on The Somme.

The bowlers and the batsmen
From the village marched away
To play their game that summer
In fields of yellow clay.
He saw them fall around him
In the white smoke of a bomb
Now the team will stay forever
By a river called The Somme.

After one, long, last reveille
And a roll-call made in vain
He met new friends with bat and ball
By the elm trees once again
But as the summer sun sank low
Casting shadows on his mind
His thoughts returned to the other game
And the team he'd left behind.

The rain beats down upon a trench
Freshly dug today
And young men walk the parapet
Their feet in yellow clay.
For seventy long years he kept
His vigil by the trees
Now reunited with the line
A soldier stands at ease.

No mortars fly above the wood
Where the high rooks wheel and turn
No rapid fire shall wake him now
Nor shrapnel tear and burn.
The years no longer matter
And age has dropped away
As a batsman takes his guard
In fields of yellow clay.

And old memories will never die
As the shadows creep along
And there never was a close of play
That summer on The Somme.

# The Dawn Chorus

The Chorus sounded in the trees
As it has since time begun.
Drifting on the summer breeze,
Heralding the morning sun.
The song hung in the eastern sky
And with the dawn moved west
Each bird spread its wings to fly
From hedgerow and from nest.

So, singers rise with joyful sound
And pass your song the world around.
You songsters come and play your tune
To the dawn and fading moon.

They settled there to join the choir
In the sun's first warming ray.
On every bush and every briar
Welcoming the break of day.
But tomorrow will the song be sung
With trees no longer there.
Will we see the morning sun
Through the acid atmosphere?

So, singers rise with joyful sound
And pass your song the world around.
You songsters come and play your tune
To the dawn and fading moon.

The dawn will never come again
No twilight reaches there.
For day and night are just the same
Beneath the neon glare.
And when the music has all gone
From barren fields of grey
We'll hear no more the morning song
That welcomed in the day.

# That Wonderful Summer

Steam trains and stocking tops
And a black Standard Ten,
Straw hats and tea shops
And waist-coated men
On horses and haywains
One long summer's day
In meadows and farm lanes
In a world slipped away.

There on the canvas
Enclosed in the scene
That wonderful summer
When I was thirteen.

Meccano, cigarette cards
And petticoat lacing,
Adverts on placards
For Scarborough so bracing.
Haystacks and hedgerows
In brushstrokes and line
Bring a view to my boyhood
Through a window in time.

There on the canvas
Enclosed in the scene
That wonderful summer
When I was thirteen.

Car seats of leather,
Phone boxes in red
While a Spitfire forever
Flies high overhead.
Sunset brings night
And a closure of play
For men dressed in white
In a world slipped away.

# The Last Hunt

He blew the horn so loud and clear
The autumn day to greet
And all the old grey Southern Hounds
Came from their homes to meet.
The huntsmen came with joyful shout
And leaping poles to gather there
To search the country round about
And find the young Jack Hare.

We crossed the ghyll at Stepping Stones
And the old grey Southern Hound
Turned Jack out at Stumble Hole
Their noses to the ground.
On crazy run Jack Hare then went
Around the Stone Pit Field
But the hounds would never leave the scent
Nor would they flag nor yield.

The hare led them a merry chase
Until the moon was seen
High above the Cider Mill
By those men in green.
From Hound House Farm to Stickle Mead
And down to Guzzel Shaw
But Lord and Squire had decreed
The hounds would run no more.

The Leaping Pole at Welland's Hill
Let young Jack Hare away
Through the valley, woods and field
To run another day.
The horn was silent in the lane
As sadly homeward bound
We knew we would not hunt again
With the old grey Southern Hound.

They ran through barley and through corn
And yellow gorse and heather,
Through the misty light of dawn
We thought they'd run forever.

## The Witch of Westcoat Wood

When wild winds wail
In the high Westcoat Wood
Tortured trees tumble and sigh.
Cascading cloud make a devil's black hood
Heaving and hellish, tormenting the sky.
Elder and Hornbeam grapple and groan.
Seagull and Raven to the valley have flown.

Cowering creatures
Hide in the barn,
Afraid of the storm and of worse.
Nearer and clearer they hear with alarm
The sound of the old witch's curse.

When westerly winds
In the wild wood wail
Thunder clouds rumble and roll.
Cackling curses borne up by the gale
Haunt the dark night so deep in its soul.
Elder and Hornbeam grapple and groan,
Seagull and Raven to the valley have flown.

Carried clear of the pine
High over Barebones
Away from the hillside borne
Now as the wild wind screeches and moans
The old witch rides out with the storm.

## The House by the Trees

Two people sit in the house on the green
Both of them lost in their very own dream.
Together they read a poem and cry.
Two people see the years rolling by.

Two people sit in the house by the park.
Together they read in the candlelit dark.
Both shed a tear as the poets relate
How two people see the changing of fate.

Two people leave the house by the trees.
Together they feel a sudden night breeze.
For, as in the poem of love turned to stone,
Two people cry, apart and alone.

## When Biggie arrived at the Wicket

When Biggie arrived at the wicket
The ball travelled far and wide
Over the roof top and into the thicket
That runs along the eastern side.
Over the boundary and over the hedge
And the hands of the fieldsmen around the edge.

If he survived first ball, they say,
He was likely to make a big score
And many's the time he saved the day
With a six or with a four.
Down through the gully and over third man
Into the bushes the red ball ran.

Then one day, off a rising ball.
As the bowler cursed and swore,
He made the biggest hit of all.
One that was never seen before.
With a mighty stroke the game was won
As he bounced the ball off the Rising Sun.

And so, once more he saved the day
With his flashing willow blade
And cricketing folk from down this way
Still talk about the stroke he made.
When from one hundred yards or more
He knocked upon the old pub door.

## Now the Singing Days are Few

Every night here in the bar
We would sing a song.
Bob Goss would start off with the Charge
And we would sing along.
He'd strike the floor there with his stick
His old dog by his side.
'That's the Balaclava Charge' he said,
'Let's re-echo it with pride.'

The thresher men would sing their song
Down in the tap-room bar.
To wash away the dust of day
They'd sing The Jolly Tar.
Jack Jordan sang Killarney
And he could sing it well.
Then every voice was raised in song
Until the closing bell.

Old Arthur raised his glass up high
As folk came through the door.
Then he sang The Gypsy Rover
And Polly on the Shore.
The Dark Eyed Sailor followed
And Dabbling in the Dew.
They were songs we seldom hear today
Now the singing days are few.

We would hear Young William Taylor
And Goodbye Dolly Gray
But that was many years ago
It's not the same today.
They've expelled the Rambling Soldier,
Something Boney couldn't do,
From the wild Banks of the Nile
Or from the Plains of Waterloo.

On a cold December night
With the wind around the door
A verse of Jim the Carter Lad
Would make us smile once more.
So why not sing that song again
And raise our voices high.
Though Arthur, Jack and Bob are gone
Their songs will never die.

They sang Banks of Green Willow
And the Foggy, Foggy Dew
Songs we seldom hear today
Now the singing days are few.

## Old Soldiers of the Line

One single voice was lifted high
As clear as sparkling wine.
A soldier's song of days gone by
From Bill the Kaiser's time.
When comrades joined in with the air
And sang farewell to Leicester Square
They woke a ghostly presence there.
Old soldiers of the line.

One old soldier's song that day
Across the bridge of time
Wiped all the bitter years away
Back to their youthful prime.
From city walls the echo strong
Came down to those who marched along
As if ten thousand sung that song.
Old soldiers of the line.

Marching into misty lore,
As the tramping echoes fade,
Go soldiers of a distant war
On this their final parade
Old voices disappeared away
Into that grey November day
And took with them the roundelay
Of soldiers from the line.

Old soldiers march again no more
As they did up to the line
And memories fade of distant war
Across the bridge of time
But in history's mist they march along
As if they were ten thousand strong
And sing forever that old song.
Old soldiers of the line.

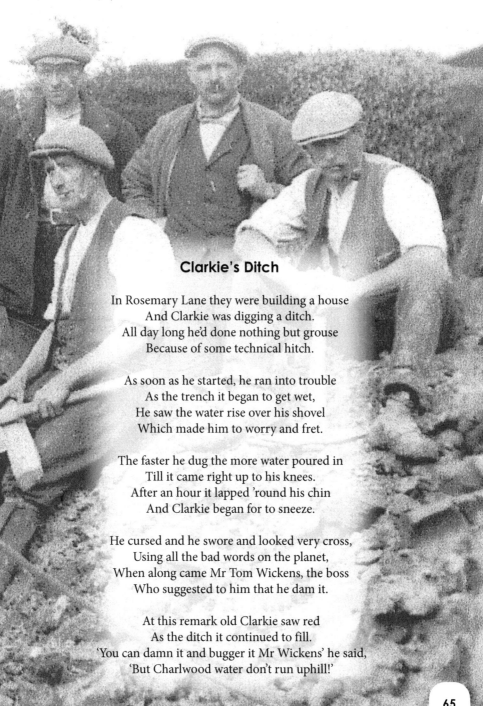

## Clarkie's Ditch

In Rosemary Lane they were building a house
And Clarkie was digging a ditch.
All day long he'd done nothing but grouse
Because of some technical hitch.

As soon as he started, he ran into trouble
As the trench it began to get wet,
He saw the water rise over his shovel
Which made him to worry and fret.

The faster he dug the more water poured in
Till it came right up to his knees.
After an hour it lapped 'round his chin
And Clarkie began for to sneeze.

He cursed and he swore and looked very cross,
Using all the bad words on the planet,
When along came Mr Tom Wickens, the boss
Who suggested to him that he dam it.

At this remark old Clarkie saw red
As the ditch it continued to fill.
'You can damn it and bugger it Mr Wickens' he said,
'But Charlwood water don't run uphill!'

## The Lurcher Dog that Walked with Me

As I came down the Welland side
My old dog raced ahead
And through the Aspen on the bank
The clouds were glowing red.
A sickle moon in silver white
Hung waiting for the April night
And there was no one else around to see
But the lurcher dog that walked with me.

By Stepping Stones I climbed the bank
Up from Welland's Gyhll
And took the floating island path
Toward the Lowfield Mill.
Then as the day prepared to die
Wild geese flew the southern sky
But in the woods the only sound
Was the stalking gipsy lurcher hound.

In Rainbow Field the dog ran free
As I heard the hour peel
And with the fading of the light
She dropped back to my heel.
Then as a distant window glowed
Dusk came down the homeward road
Casting shadows all around
Where I walked the gipsy lurcher hound.

As I passed by the cattle shed
I saw the clouds had cleared
And high above the Old Grub Field
The first bright star appeared.
By the gate awhile I stayed
To see the crimson sunset fade
And there was no one else around to see
But the lurcher dog that walked with me.

## Go and get Tula

'Go and get Tula!'
The cry went up
All around the ground.
'Go and get Tula
The Spaniel pup.
There's a ball that can't be found'.

'Go and get Tula,'
The fielders say,
'Because we have searched in vain.
Go and get Tula,
For we can't play
'Till she finds the ball again.'

'Go and get Tula
So she may run
Down where the brackens grow,
Go and bring Tula
To the place
Where the searchers seldom go.'

'Go and get Tula!'
The call rings out
As they raise up high the score.
'Go and get Tula!'
But in vain they shout
For Tula is no more.

## Sweet Birdsong

I thought that when the Jumbo came
The sweet birdsong would not remain.
That thrush, in fear, away would soar
At the mighty engine's roar.
Leaving gardens and the trees
To the fumes that cloak the breeze.

A One-Eleven screams on by.
It rocks the ground and shakes the sky
And a Jumbo blasts into the blue
Rattling doors and windows too
But a blackbird struts upon my lawn
Treating both with equal scorn.

The thrush and he now sing together
As though it were the first day ever.
Louder and more sweeter yet
Determined to out-sing the jet.
And in the Jumbo's smoky track
I heard the robin roaring back.

## That Last Fraction of a Mile

The young men of the village
Walked with you all the way
Along the old stone path
On that December day.
Remembering your loving ways
And your tender smile
They said they wished to walk with you
That last fraction of a mile.

That last fraction of a mile
In a long, long journey run
Saw tears upon the grey stone
Dry in the winter sun.
Recalling how you dried their tears
And cured their sorrows too
They were walking with a solemn tread
And caring now for you.

They said that they would miss you
When they left you at the door
Where you had stood with your young man
Some sixty years before.
Then, your journey it was over
And you were safely home
The young men of the village
Walked back again alone.

## The Village Heroes

See the village heroes of twenty years ago
Standing on the touchline, cloth caps in a row,
Shouting out instructions that no one really hears
And secretly regretting the passing of the years.

Tired old village heroes of forty years ago
Sitting by the flat screen, fire bars aglow,
Following a game with the sound turned up
And dreaming of the day they nearly won the cup.

See today's young stranger out on the field of play,
Having driven down from London, many miles away,
To follow in the footsteps of a hundred seasons played
And be a sporting hero when village goals are made.

They who should be heroes of the village saga
Gather round the fruit machine with their pints of lager.
Not for them the winning goal from the volleyed shot
They dream of four bars in a row and tonight's jackpot.

Faded old time heroes of eighteen ninety-nine
Gathered by the goalpost all in their ghostly prime
Hope to see the village men once more chase the leather
And one day win the silver cup and hold it high forever.

## It was there I saw the Unicorns

It was there I saw the Unicorns
A year ago, last May
Bursting through a sunbeam
On an overcast spring day.
They stepped to left and skipped to right
And halted there as one
To be followed to that very spot
By a single ray of sun.

I know I saw the Unicorns!
Or was it just a dream?
Stepping right and skipping left
A few yards from the stream.
They raised their heads together
And looked me in the eye
Then challenged me to look again
As I was passing by.

The others paused to take a look
Before going on their way
But did they see the Unicorns?
I don't know, they didn't say.
Some returned next morning,
I supposed they weren't quite sure
But if you doubt the Unicorns
They will dance for you no more.

Did you see the Unicorns?
Each with a snow-white mane.
For if you did then come next spring
They'll dance for you again.

## Now that the Cowman's Gone

Today we heard that he had gone
Away from us too soon.
That he had sung his farewell song
And played his final tune.
The poplars stand in mournful line
And as the sun goes down
The last leaf of the summertime
Is falling to the ground.

The cows are coming home tonight
Without his cheerful song.
The music with the summer fades
Now that the cowman's gone.

With that last leaf of summer came
The winter dark and chill
And days would never be the same
With no song upon the hill.
For he has fallen like the leaves
In his October song
And silent stand the magic keys
His fingers danced along.

But the grey of late November
Will turn around to spring
When we sit and we remember
The song he used to sing.
And so, my friends be of good cheer
And let us sing his song
He'd rather that than shed a tear
Now that the cowman's gone.

The cows are coming home tonight
Without his cheerful song.
The music with the summer fades
Now that the cowman's gone.

# Please Scatter My Bails

Last Saturday night as the light it grew dim
The village was playing at cricket.
With an hour to play and the last man in
Old Katie stood firm at the wicket.
He blocked the view because of his size.
No one could see 'keeper nor slips
As crouched in the shadows of his massive thighs
They attempted to peer round his hips.

The bowler bore down with a menacing run
And old Katie lashed out with his bat
But he missed every time and the boundary rung
To the other team's cries of 'how's that?'
But the umpire all the appeals did ignore
As the willow enjoyed a fine breeze.
'How can I hope to see leg before
When his belly hangs over his knees?'

Still Katie bore the sickening thumps
'Till his body was all black and bruised
But the umpire never caught sight of the stumps
And he scratched his head most confused.
At last, Katie said, 'Now I don't want to trouble you
But it was better it was all cut and dried.
If the ball hits my belly it's called L.B.W.
And if it hits my backside it's a wide.'

At the very next ball Katie started to run
Vibrating the ground with his feet.
He broke his duck, his wrist and his thumb
When he fell to the ground in a heap.
The sun it went down behind his great frame
Bringing the shadows of night
And the umpire had to abandon the game
Because of the pain and bad light.

The door opened up in the pub 'cross the way
And old Katie cried, 'Why am I here?
Please scatter my bails, let's call it a day.
I would rather be drinking my beer.'

## Daniel's Challenge

Daniel Butcher was a mighty man
A challenge he could not resist.
As mine-host of the village inn
He kept order with his fist.
Day or night 'twas his delight
To toe the line and have a fight
And strong men came from miles about
But he proved the best without a doubt.

Now Daniel had a pony fine
That pulled his cart around.
The animal was his pride and joy
For a better one could not be found.
But one dark day two men arrived
And for a joke they both contrived
To challenge Daniel fair and square
To lift his pony up the stair.

Daniel then the challenge took
And the prize was set
As a gallon of his best brown beer
If he won the bet.
The village heard a mighty roar
As the pony left the floor
And to the amazement of those there
He carried it up the winding stair.

But eager to possess his prize
Before the men walked up the street
He left the pony in the room
Where it ate three blankets and a sheet!
Daniel's wife came home from town
Saw ragged curtains hanging down
But when she saw what was on the bed
It was then that Daniel's wife saw red!

She thundered down into the bar
And saw her husband lazing.
'Why was there a pony, pray,
In the bedroom grazing?'
Receiving then no explanation
She finished off his reputation
With a solid right to Daniel's jaw
Which sent him tumbling to the floor!

# Much Squirming in the Pew

For centuries there seemed to be
Much squirming in the pew
And unofficial watering
Of the ancient hollow yew.
The Saxon used the bushes
Normans hid behind the wall
And Puritans walked for many miles
Just to answer nature's call,

For the service lasts forever
And the sermon seems so slow
When you want to spend a penny
And there is no place to go.

Extremities were frozen
In winter's ice and frost
So Quakers stayed at home to pray
Whilst other's legs were crossed.
From pulpit high the Parson saw
Discomfort of the Squire,
Contortions of the Parish Clerk,
Red faces in the choir.

For the service lasts forever
And the sermon seems so slow
When you want to spend a penny
And there is no place to go.

For centuries there seemed to be
No snoozes and no snores
But it's hard to get your forty winks
When you are forced to go outdoors.
But redundancy is on its way
For the bush and for the tree
And pray we may relax one day
In a parochial W.C.

## The Free Men of Charlwood

From these fields the ceorls went forth
In defence of cott and byre
To meet the savage of the north
In paths of smoke and fire.
At Barebones legend still remains
Of battle with the fearsome Danes
When red clad girls denied a haven
To the black, defeated raven.

From these farms marched out a band
In defiant insurrection
When Earl Suffolk tried his hand
At murder and corruption.
Tom Jordan cried for liberty
And Saunders for no tyranny
Before a rusty sword on Dover's strand
Brought justice back into the land.

To this church a sailor came
When Boney plotted our defeat
Vernon Jackson was his name
And he sailed with the fleet
That boldly fought as Nelson died
And scattered Frenchmen on the tide.
Returning then to Charlwood home
An Admiral hero of the foam.

At this wicket the Parson's son
Displayed his skill with bat and ball
But then exchanged them for a gun
In answer to his country's call.
Playing then a different game
Tommy-gun Thompson earned his name.
For valour bold and deeds supreme
He won a Knighthood from his Queen.

From these cottages the men went out
To Flanders and to Spain
To tame the bear at The Redoubt
And win the day at Alamein.
At the Somme and Passchendaele
They fought and died in muddy hell.
Their names are listed on the stone
In the churchyard of their village home.

For a thousand summers in this lane
With liberty the prize
From battle with invading Dane
To nineteen forty's angry skies,
Before squire, lord or jackboot heel
The Charlwood man refused to kneel,
Defying pomp and tyranny
A village man but always free.

## When Apted was in Hold

One dark and rainy winter's night
When villains roamed throughout the land
And lonely travellers stood in fright
As smugglers hauled their contraband
Bold Blanchard went a 'riding out
Against the winter's rage
With two brave men close by his side
To put Tom Apted in The Cage.

As Constable of the parish he
Held the warrant in his hand
With trusty sword hung by his knee
In lawful majesty so grand.
Tom was taken to The Hold
In custody without a fight
To await the journey to the judge
At the coming of the morning light.

To guard the prisoner, they stayed near
At the Half Moon Inn, not far away.
Drinking wine and well mulled beer
Until the breaking of the day.
'Another jug of ale kind sir,
If I may make so bold.'
Such a merry time was had by all
When Apted was in hold.

When, at last, the dawn did creep
Across the common from the east
It found the men all fast asleep
In consequence of their liquid feast.
On bare stone floor without a bed
The prisoner languished in his cell
While constable with cradled head
Complained of feeling none too well.

They slept until midday arrived
Then food and drink were bought.
They drunk until too late to ride
To Epsom and the court.
In the old Half Moon close by the church
The happy drunkards rolled
For two whole days of merriment
When Apted was in hold.

They came, at last, before the beak
And evidence the judge could see.
The constable too ill to speak
And Apted was set free.
Bold Blanchard claimed a fortune
In expenses, so I'm told.
For keeping law and order
When Apted was in hold.

# A Yellow Dog Slept in the Sun

A six-year-old played in the yard
And a yellow dog slept in the sun.
My father was home from the war
And the worrying days were all done.

The bonfire crackled and burned
Then nearly faded away.
I laughed at the smoke and the flame
For this was my happiest day.

My father was home from the war
And although the days were still hard
A six-year-old played in the sun
And a yellow dog slept in the yard.

The smell of smoke from the wood
And roast from the old kitchen range
We were a family once more
And nothing would ever now change.

My father was home from the war
No more to follow the drum
And the smoke drifted over the yard
Where a yellow dog slept in the sun.

## Lord Kitchener's Men

Lord Kitchener's men had answered the call
Of the finger that pointed from every wall.
Old George stepped forward to join the line
To fight for his King and to serve his time.
He marched away to do his bit
To the steady beat of the regiment's drum
But had to prove he was fighting fit
Before they set him on the Hun.

The doctor saw George upon Aldershot Heath
But reported to him that he had bad teeth.
George gave a cough and touched his toes
And listened to the diagnose.
'The first thing I will have to mention,
Before you meet the German foe,
The top right does need some attention
But the rest, I fear, will have to go!'

'You see old chap,' the doctor said,
'There's not a good one in your head.
We really cannot let you loose
Upon the Hun without a tooth.
We want an army fit for the wars
A full set for each of the men.'
'I've come to battle the buggers,' said George,
'Not to bloody well eat them!'

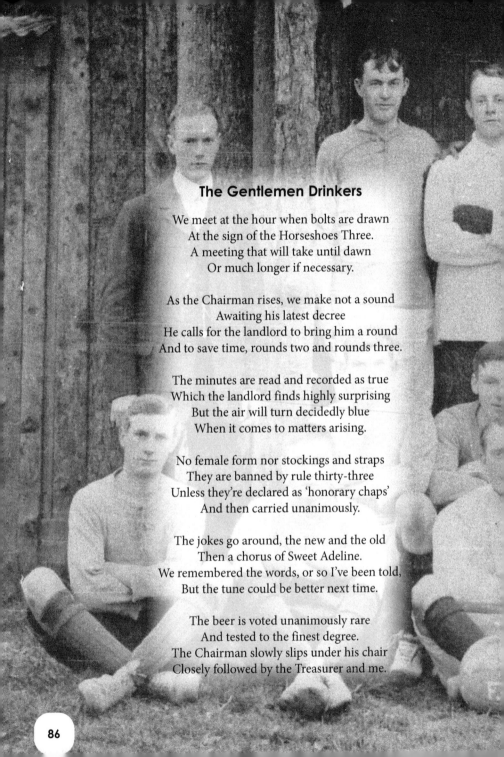

## The Gentlemen Drinkers

We meet at the hour when bolts are drawn
At the sign of the Horseshoes Three.
A meeting that will take until dawn
Or much longer if necessary.

As the Chairman rises, we make not a sound
Awaiting his latest decree
He calls for the landlord to bring him a round
And to save time, rounds two and rounds three.

The minutes are read and recorded as true
Which the landlord finds highly surprising
But the air will turn decidedly blue
When it comes to matters arising.

No female form nor stockings and straps
They are banned by rule thirty-three
Unless they're declared as 'honorary chaps'
And then carried unanimously.

The jokes go around, the new and the old
Then a chorus of Sweet Adeline.
We remembered the words, or so I've been told,
But the tune could be better next time.

The beer is voted unanimously rare
And tested to the finest degree.
The Chairman slowly slips under his chair
Closely followed by the Treasurer and me.

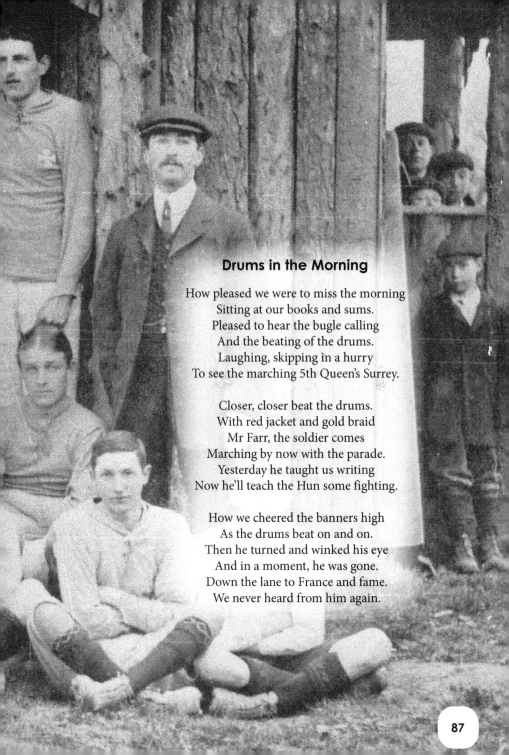

## Drums in the Morning

How pleased we were to miss the morning
Sitting at our books and sums.
Pleased to hear the bugle calling
And the beating of the drums.
Laughing, skipping in a hurry
To see the marching 5th Queen's Surrey.

Closer, closer beat the drums.
With red jacket and gold braid
Mr Farr, the soldier comes
Marching by now with the parade.
Yesterday he taught us writing
Now he'll teach the Hun some fighting.

How we cheered the banners high
As the drums beat on and on.
Then he turned and winked his eye
And in a moment, he was gone.
Down the lane to France and fame.
We never heard from him again.

# The Bright Path

I wandered along the bright path
Where the bloom of the wild rose fair
Entwined with the line of a soft summer song
And hung on the scented air.

It waited for me by the high field
Where the blue corn bends in the breeze
And ripples and waves at the edge of the wood
Broke on the line of dark trees.

Golden shafts came down in the dark wood
Into the emerald shade
But the song lingered high in the sapphire sky
Where the top most branches swayed.

But time is not long on the bright path
To seek out the song and the flower
The rhymes drift away across the blue corn
And the bloom fades away with the hour.

The bloom fades away with the hour
And the hours drift into the days
And along with the song of the summer
Disappears in the sweet autumn haze.

I wish near the end of the bright path
Where the rain beats down on my door
To hear once again the soft summer song
As I walk by the wild rose once more.

## Waiting for the Ferry

At the end of the jetty dark waters are high,
Still, deep and reflecting every star in the sky.
Across the cold fjord where horizons should be
The sky, earth and mountains merge with the sea.

The Milky Way fills the black satin dome
With lights on black water as I stand here alone.
Like a traveller in space, the stars all around,
In an ebony silence, a vacuum of sound.

Out here, in the void, time has no meaning
For a solitary man and a million stars gleaming.
In a cone of deep peace, the hour slips away
And a million years are but a day.

But time hurries back as ripples draw near
The bright stars are fractured at the end of the pier.
An amplified voice booms into the Heaven,
'The ferry to Allsund leaves at eight thirty-seven'.

## Graffiti in the Blue

So, you have daubed the old grey stone!
Where names are listed of 'the Few'.
To make a statement of your own
But is this the best that you could do?
In content and artistic flair
Your strokes are bold and true
But in no way does your work compare
With their graffiti in the blue.

They too were filled with youthful rage
Their faces wan and pale
As they left their mark on history's page
With twisting vapour trail.
In disrespect they carved their names
Above the iron gale
In oil and smoke and yellow flames
They died in hill and dale.

They daubed the sky to save the world
And just like you they stood alone.
Their smudged graffiti rose and swirled
In smoky grey and blood red tone.
They dared to act by light of day
And deface the skies of home
So that, one day, you could have your say.
(Their names are listed on the stone.)

## The Mariner's Tale

The midday tide it came and went
Too fast for us and so we spent
Twelve hours on mud condemned to lie
While the Medway river hurried by.

Old Mummery swore when we missed the tide
And cursed the water flowing wide
Of the mud that stopped Felicity
From heading for the estuary.

Then a drop of grog for the land-locked sailors
And a chorus song about the whalers.
They never made mistakes like us.
We should have caught the green-line bus.

Only ten hours more and the tide comes back
According to Reed's Almanac.
We should have read that first I fear
By now we'd be at Margate Pier.

So once more we read the news
Times, Observer and 'The Screws'.
Watch this supplement float down
Passed the bridge to Chatham Town.

Now, at last midnight is here
The boat is floating almost clear.
Ben's in the water, mud to the knee
One more push and then we're free.

Free as the lonely sea and the sky
Cap'n Ben Newton, old Mummery and I.
We'll sail away on the tidal flood
Far from that murky Medway mud.

## The Little Stove at Vardebu

I travelled north from London Town,
Where the street lamps spread their gold
On autumn leaves of red and brown,
To a land so white and cold.
But the mountains blazed at sunset,
Pure gold against the blue,
And promised me more treasures yet
As I climbed up to Vardebu.

The Ruppe sang a lonely song
As she flew the silver lake
And satin clouds were blown along
With diamonds in their wake.
Then came the crystal light of dawn
That chilled my body through
To be banished by the golden warm
Of the little stove at Vardebu.

When I recall those Artic gales
That around the cabin blew
I'll remember when my spirit fails
How the candle flame held true,
And if a wish for wealth I make
When my sad days are few
I shall think again of the silver lake
And the golden glow of Vardebu.

# The Day of the Numbers

I dreamed of the day of the numbers
Of figures and symbols and slots
The computers that counted the slumbers
With sensors that lined children's cots.

Silently waiting they waited
Men all stood in a row
Numbered from one to five thousand
Waiting for data to flow.

One to five thousand the same
With faces eight, nine and grey
Francis, Richard and Robert's the name
It's numbers that count here today.

Somewhere a window is open.
A bird sings high in the blue
A light of recognition springs to the eyes
Of number one thousand and two.

A river a mountain a lake and a wood
A bird in a long-ago dream
When men and women lived as they would
Before the computing machine.

Love of a girl, laugh of a child
The sun on the grass and the seas
The wind in the hair and a forest so wild
But now they have numbered the trees.

One thousand and two remember that day
Of a song and a tankard of beer.
Software and updates you must now obey
With prefix and password to prove that you're here.

## When the Terror Time had Passed

That spring time by the beech trees
When the terror time had passed.
He felt the gentle southern breeze
That followed winter's blast.
For the bitter war was over
Bringing peace and hope at last.

A warrior in a peaceful world
Where no bugles call
Saw the yellow buds unfurled
Beside the forest pool
And when the birds sang out with joy
He heard the chorus rise and fall.

The man who had defied the foe
Recalled his doubts and fears
Of the desperate battle's ebb and flow
Throughout those troubled years.
He saw the rose in wild bloom
And his eyes were filled with tears.

Weeping in this peaceful bliss
After years of bomb and flame,
'To think we nearly lost all this,'
Said the hero of great fame,
'Only I can tell the tale
Of just how close we really came.'

## Angle Tarn

The mountain dreamed.
A seagull screamed
From glowering rocks
Out into the swirling cloud
and darkening shroud
Of evening.
Far below by the lake
The reeds grew high
And shuddered at the seagull's cry.

Through the haze
Of the blues and greys
Of those high and lonely hills
A sudden light on
the towering height
Of Black Crags
Lingered briefly then was lost.
Hidden in mist and grey disguised
Beneath the sullen, stormy skies.

The clouds rolled down
From Langdale's crown
Dismissing that last ray of sun
That danced and played as
it shone and made
So bright a gem.
I scanned the sombre hills around,
The shimmering vision to regain
But all I saw was the mist and the
steady, steady slate grey rain.

# When Dublin Town Lay Sleeping

Somewhere a whistle played
As we walked the street along.
Having raised a glass with many a friend
In merry tune and song.
As Dublin Town lay sleeping
The music lingered on.

We crossed the River Liffey
Beneath O'Connell's gaze
Attempting to locate the tune
But it came from many ways.
The silver notes soon filled the air
With songs from former days.

He crossed our path at Jervis Street.
I recognised the tune.
And we fell right in beside him
At The Rising of the Moon.
Then came O'Delaigh's ancient air
The song Eileen Aroon.

His long dark hair was flowing
Stirring in the breeze
Black coat buttoned tight
From his beard down to his knees.
His tune around re-echoing
Down to the Liffey Quays.

Of us he seemed quite unaware
As he eyed the road ahead.
With silver whistle to his lips
Not a single word was said.
Down unknown ways we followed
Where the magic whistle led.

In Boulavogue we joined in song
As with Fields of Athenry
And at the Square old Skibbereen
Was lifted to the sky.
And when he played the Ninety-Eight
We heard old Wexford cry.

It was in a cobbled courtyard
Where the music stopped
Beside a wooden door
That appeared to be well locked
In silence there we waited
While the whistle player knocked.

The door swung open wide
Onto a dark and smoke-filled hall
Where rough and bearded drinking men
Sat around the wall.
In the gloom a fiddler played
The Star of Donegal.

We heard a whistle playing,
From where we never knew,
Among those rough and bearded men
With their dark brown brew,
A song about an Easter time
In Dublin's foggy dew.

Melodeon and fiddle
And poem followed song,
Until dawn's early morning light
We drank and sung along.
When Dublin Town lay sleeping
The music lingered on.

## The White Doves Change Direction

Over Great High Field where nothing moves
In hedgerow or in tree
I hurry home to shelter
While there's light enough to see.
Yesterday in blue skies
They flew the golden corn
Now the white doves fly for cover
At the coming of the storm.

The white doves change direction
In a slate grey southern sky,
With the pale sunlight on the wing
The last beams fade and die.

From haystack out to hillside
All colour drains away
And silent fields are turning
To sepia tones and grey.
No sunlight now upon the wing
Of the white dove in the glade
Where the air hangs hot and heavy
In the storm clouds darkening shade.

The white doves change direction
In a slate grey southern sky
With the pale sunlight on the wing
The last beams fade and die.

And Great High Field is waiting
For the thunder and the rain
To sweep away the grey skies
And move the leaf again.
But still the air hangs heavy
And nothing makes a sound
As the white doves fly for cover
Above the stubbled ground.

### Shivery Dark Halloween

Isn't it fun to shriek in the dark
Like a banshee with blood curdling yells?
To scare poor old folk in a long black cloak
With Dracula fangs in our mouths.

Isn't it fun to laugh all the time
As we frighten each other to death?
With stories of witches which have us in stitches
And leave us all gasping for breath.

Isn't it fun to be looking so scary
That you shiver and shake in your boots?
To be creeping like ghouls in lonely old halls
Dressed in terrible skeleton suits.

Isn't it fun with the dark trees all bare.
And the frightened moon staring between?
To be out in the night and to be such a sight
When it's shivery dark Halloween.

# Unchanged

We were young and carefree
In fields of autumn gold.
We thought we'd live forever
But now we are grown old.

He was old and shook his stick
Like a man deranged
But with a twinkle in his eye.
Still he has not changed.

By shot and flame disfigured
In another time and place,
Condemned to live his life
Within an old man's face.

Fifty years have seen us age
With faces lined and grey
But he, unchanged, with twinkling eye
Still shakes his stick at day.

# The Sweet Silver Song

I welcomed the wind on its westerly wings
That through the wheat whispered its wandering way
But I search in vain for a lark that sings
Over daises that danced on a hot summer day.

The bee beckoned by the blossom of briar
Buzzes beneath the bramble and bloom
While the sweet silver song rises higher and higher
I scan the sky for the source of the tune.

Borne by the breezes that blow in the bushes
Closer and clearer came the clarion call.
Above, in the blue, I see swallow and thrushes
But of the sweet summer songster nothing at all.

The tune tumbled down cascading on corn
And golden green grasses soon to be hay.
Then the sweet summer song was suddenly borne
Over daises that danced in fields far away.

# Seven Geese are Flying

Seven geese are flying
Above the rainbow's crest,
Out from where the day is dying,
To the sunset and the west.
In a dark and stormy sky
Seven geese are flying high.

Seven geese in twilight glow
Fly through the April rain
Across the spectrum of the bow
On wings of feathered flame.
Then, as one the wild geese cry
As the colours fade and die.

A rainbow and the geese together
Bring joy into the day.
A moment that is lost forever
As the rainbow slips away
And like an arrow straight and true
Seven geese fly out of view.

# So Late in the Town

The hour is lonely
The night has turned chill.
The first signs of morning
Creep over the hill.
He sees the moon high
As he saw the sun down
When she went out dancing
So late in the town.

Sleep is a stranger
As the clock it strikes four
There's no sound of her tread
Or her key in the door.
Into the room
Comes the cold light of morn
But she's down in the town
And dancing 'till dawn.

From his window he sees
The fields that lie bare.
The dark road is silent
For nobody's there.
There's mist in the high wood
And dew on the lawn
But she's down in the town
And dancing 'till dawn.

The pale moon is sinking
Behind the dark pine
But the bright lights are where
Her sparkling eyes shine.
He hears the wind whisper
Through the leaves turning brown
That she's gone out dancing
So late in the town.

# As Right as the Day

When the fields were set free from winter's cold grip
We wandered down Ladylands way.
Harbingers of springtime had been let slip
And we were as right as the day.

High on the top of Colley Stile crest
Where the lapwings they tumble and play
A gentle breeze came from out of the west
Bringing the warmth of the day.

The hedgerows were touched by young Jack in the Green
When he chanced to pass by this way
And down on the banks where the willow trees lean
We were as right as the day.

Then out of Long Copse we spotted the hare
And the dogs they were up and away
Over meadows and ditches they chased without care
As they ran the length of the day.

The white hawthorn gleamed and the daffodil shone
And we were as right as the day.
We recalled words of an old summer song
For springtime was not far away.

When the fields were set free from winter's cold grip
We wandered down Ladylands way.
My hand in your hand I chanced to let slip
And we were as right as the day.

## Lonely Places

He had loved the sun
On high and lonely places
When plunging streams were cool and fresh
And sprayed upon rock faces.
He found magic in the trees
And tall grasses on the hill
When stirred by gentle summer breeze
Of evening.

He roamed along the ancient ways
Through ivy, grass and creeper
Where crow flies by, alone, above
And peace could be no deeper.
Old songs shivered down his spine
And legends came alive
When old men sat and sang of time
And days gone by.

To lovely girls he'd said goodbye
In the early morning after.
Known the comradeship of men
Sealed in song and laughter.
But now content in fireside seat
He sings along with her
She who made his life complete
Far from lonely places.

## Return to the Bright Path

If you should discover the bright path
You may find a song waiting there.
Where the barley blows and the scent of the rose
Still hangs on the summer air.

I searched for that song on the bright path
By the great high oak and the beech
But it drifted away on a summer's day
And stayed just out of my reach.

I lost the song on the bright path
So many long years ago.
To recall it again I tried but in vain
When the fields were covered in snow.

But it waits for you by the high field
Where the barley yet bends in the breeze
And waves that are borne along the blue corn
Still caress the line of dark trees.

So, go searching along the bright path
In the soft, sweet scented air
Then sing me the song that waited so long
Down by the wild rose fair.

## Your Golden Summer Gown

Tomorrow you will dress in red
And autumn shades of brown
But today you look so lovely
In your golden summer gown.
As I stand here in the barley
And watch the twilight fall
The evening mist comes with the moon
To bring your silver shawl.

As harvest time draws nigh
The hedgerows laden down
With berries and with flowers
Make ribbons for your gown.
They tumble down the distant hill
From a saucy bonnet green
Where blackthorn meets the barley
And oak and ash tree lean.

When the hillside wore the white
And winter winds blew cold
You rested there just for a while
To dream of green and gold
And when you woke in sunshine
The soft warm April rain
Returned the colour to your gown
And woke the fields again.

I wandered through the springtime
Beneath the buds new born
And on into the summer
Through fields of golden corn.
Then sunshine through the bright leaves
Made necklaces of green
To lay upon your summer gown,
The fairest ever seen.

Your summer gown lay gleaming
Beneath the clear blue sky
From hill to shining distant hill
As harvest time draws nigh.

## The Beggar House Reel

Remember that night long ago
When we danced the Beggar House Reel
Down through the orchards of Greenings
At the foot of Beggar House Hill.
The sun was low in the Westwood
And scattered the orchard with gold
When I swung you around in the last dance
To keep out the coming night cold.

And the old songs that night flowed like wine
As we stood by the fire's rosy glow
With the fiddler marking the time
For the dancers of long, long ago.

But now the dancers have gone.
They've gone with the fiddlers bow.
No longer can we hear the old song
And the orchard is covered in snow.
Many months I waited for summer
For the songs and the music again
When I'd swing you around in the Beggar House Reel
And we'd forget about winter and rain.

And the old songs that night flowed like wine
As we stood by the fire's rosy glow
With the fiddler marking the time
For the dancers of long, long ago.

And now the hill it stands silent
Where the wild and the wet grasses grow
And gone is the Beggar House Reel
We danced in those days long ago.
But the songs, the music and laughter
Still echo to me down the lane
And although it's fifty years after
I can see you there dancing again.

113

# Sixty Years Ago, This June

Sixty years ago, this June
We danced the bonfire round
In a pageant of past glory
On the Recreation Ground.
We recalled the Great Armada
And battle with the Dane
As we gathered there that summer
To welcome in her reign.

Ten long years passed on by
The sixties now were swinging
And from the Sun and old Half Moon
We heard the sound of singing.
High up in the Parish Hall
A portrait of The Queen
And Jim Davies won the hundred yards
That summer on the green.

As bunting fluttered overhead
We drank our wine and beer
As merrily we raised a glass
To toast her silver year
But as we sang God Save the Queen
There came a mighty roar
And we were forced to fight again
Bulldozers at the door.

Many years flew quickly by
And silver turned to gold
We raised our glasses once again
To a reign now growing old.
But gold then turned to diamond bright
And still we may be seen
The Charlwood men whose toast will be
God save our gracious Queen.

Let everyone now raise a glass
And drink a toast with me,
Elizabeth Regina
Jubilee, Jubilee, Jubilee.

# A Village Man

A village man both born and bred
He knew the country ways.
Remembering things, the old folk said
And stories of the long-gone days.
At the farm in thirty-three,
Whilst working on the land,
He helped Mary plant a tree,
A Cedar, now so strong and grand.

In nineteen forty Europe burned
And he went away to war.
Five years later he returned
To take the field once more.
Then we really saw him play,
Such bowling now is seldom seen,
And old men still recall the day
He took nine wickets on the green.

Around the bar at dominoes
And darts he won the game
And still, in pubs, the dusty rows
Of trophies bear his name.
There in the walls he built so high
Future men will see
A testament to hand and eye.
A skilful man was he.

At fisticuffs when he was young
He'd fight and not back down
Just like the time he held a gun
Defending King and Crown.
'Easily led but never druv'
A village man but free.
Don't drive him now, good Lord above,
Let him be led by thee.

## The Re-Union

At last the mud shall have him
After all the years
At last he goes to meet once more
His comrades and his peers.
They fell and fell and fell and fell
Four hundred thousand strong
In a clinging, yellow nightmare
Where now the poppies throng.

With sons and grandsons round him
Bareheaded in the rain
He rests once more with valiant men
In yellow mud again.
But the mud they pile upon him
Is not that tortured loam
But the peaceful English earth
Of his beloved home.

No more the screams shall haunt him
From a time so long ago
When friends and comrades marched to death
Where now the poppies grow.
His garden just two fields away
And the house where he was born
Shall hear Reveille by church bells
Throughout the years at dawn.

### The Jewels of the Night

What have they done to the jewels of the night?
To Orion the Moon and the Plough.
The weary traveller's old guiding light
Comes from another source now.

The glare through the trees at the edge of the field
Draws a curtain on night with a harsh yellow shield
And over the hedge comes a dull foggy glow
Of a sodium haze where the moon once hung low.

The swathe of black satin I gazed on when young
That twinkled and shone with bright diamonds of night
From hedgerow to hillside so carelessly strung
Now so far away from my sight.

And there in the barn an owl yearns for the night
And the darkness he knew long ago
He's patiently waiting to take his last flight
Through the wheat and the barley, the stars all aglow.

## The Dancers

Did I see them dancing
Off into the west
From Blackcap near Mount Harry
To below the Bignor Crest?
They crossed the bridge at Greatham
Each with a graceful bound
And in the east the stars came out
When old Mount Harry frowned.

Did they go a'dancing
In a copse below the ring
When rowdy rooks ceased calling
To let the nightingales sing?
Skipping down West Burton street
Close by the Roman grounds
Did they dance the hours away
That night there on the Downs?

Did they go a'dancing
Beside the silver stream
When all of Sussex slumbered?
Or was it just a dream?
When they stopped to bow their heads
The Arun made no sound.
The moon shone down on Amberley
And old Mount Harry frowned.

## Old Arky's Toast

We'll drink to the downfall of tyrants
We'll drink to Christ the Lord
And to each of the twelve apostles
Who preached his holy word.
We'll drink to the saints and martyrs
In the dismal days of yore
And whenever our glasses are empty
We'll remember one saint more.

We'll drink a health to the King my boys
We'll drink a health to the Queen
And here's to the Royal Princes
Wherever they are seen
We'll drink to the Dukes and Duchesses
And all the loyal men
And whenever our glasses are empty
We will fill them up again.

And now we'll drink to the ladies
We'll drink to all their charms
We'll drink to the pleasures we do find
When we are in their arms.
We'll hold them very tight, my boys,
But we will make it clear
It's goodbye on the day when they do say
They will keep us from our beer.

We'll drink to the master and mistress
At their glorious harvest feast.
We'll raise our glasses high, my boys,
To the strength of malt and yeast.
We'll drink a health to the landlord
And his beer so strong and fine
And we hope that he forgets to shout
When it comes to closing time.

## The Annual Village Ball

The heavy metal sounds beat out
And shake the Parish Hall
Where once they glided in a waltz
At the Annual Village Ball.
The whispered message soft and low
Was answered with a sigh
When they held each other tight
In those days gone by.

But now, with banging drum and bass,
They leap and shake about.
The lover's message is unheard
Or answered with a shout.
But beneath the portrait of the Queen
Ghostly figures dance once more.
As rocking music fades away
They glide across the floor.

And when the last waltz has been danced
They all stand up and sing
One final loud rendition
Of God Save our Gracious King.
But alas the last waltz is no more
In this heavy metal scene
And someone's drawn a black moustache
On the portrait of the Queen.

## The Last Rehearsal

Roll up, roll up and see the show.
It's the drama of the year
And sing the old songs merrily
With fish and chips and beer.
Mr Tudgay's thumping at the keys
All white and black and brown
Where Hazel spilt the coffee
When she went tumbling down.

And we'll sing bluebirds over
If we can find the key
And a long, long trail a winding
Tomorrow wait and see.

And we'll sing bluebirds over
If we can find the key
And a long, long trail a winding
Tomorrow wait and see.

The conjurer's got more rabbit
Than it takes to do his trick
And Adrian Wright is searching
For his powder and lipstick.
Someone ought to mend the stage
Before we all fall through
But Captain Green goes on and on
About the north of Katmandu.

Mr Noble's waiting in the wings
In his safety hat
That well known, almost foremost,
Banjo playing acrobat,
He will soon amaze us all
With his daring flight
And although he's never done it yet
It'll be alright on the night.

Now Hazel's singing up on stage
Dressed up like Betty Grable.
By the middle of the second half
She'll be underneath the table.
For the prompter's found another crate
Of medium white wine
And just like Hazel up on stage
He's forgotten the next line.

Roll up, roll up and see the show.
It's the drama of the year
And sing the old songs merrily
With fish and chips and beer.
It's the good old Charlwood Players
Says the poster on the wall
And tonight, they tread the dodgy boards
Down at the village hall.

And we'll sing bluebirds over
If we can find the key
And a long, long trail a winding
Tomorrow wait and see.

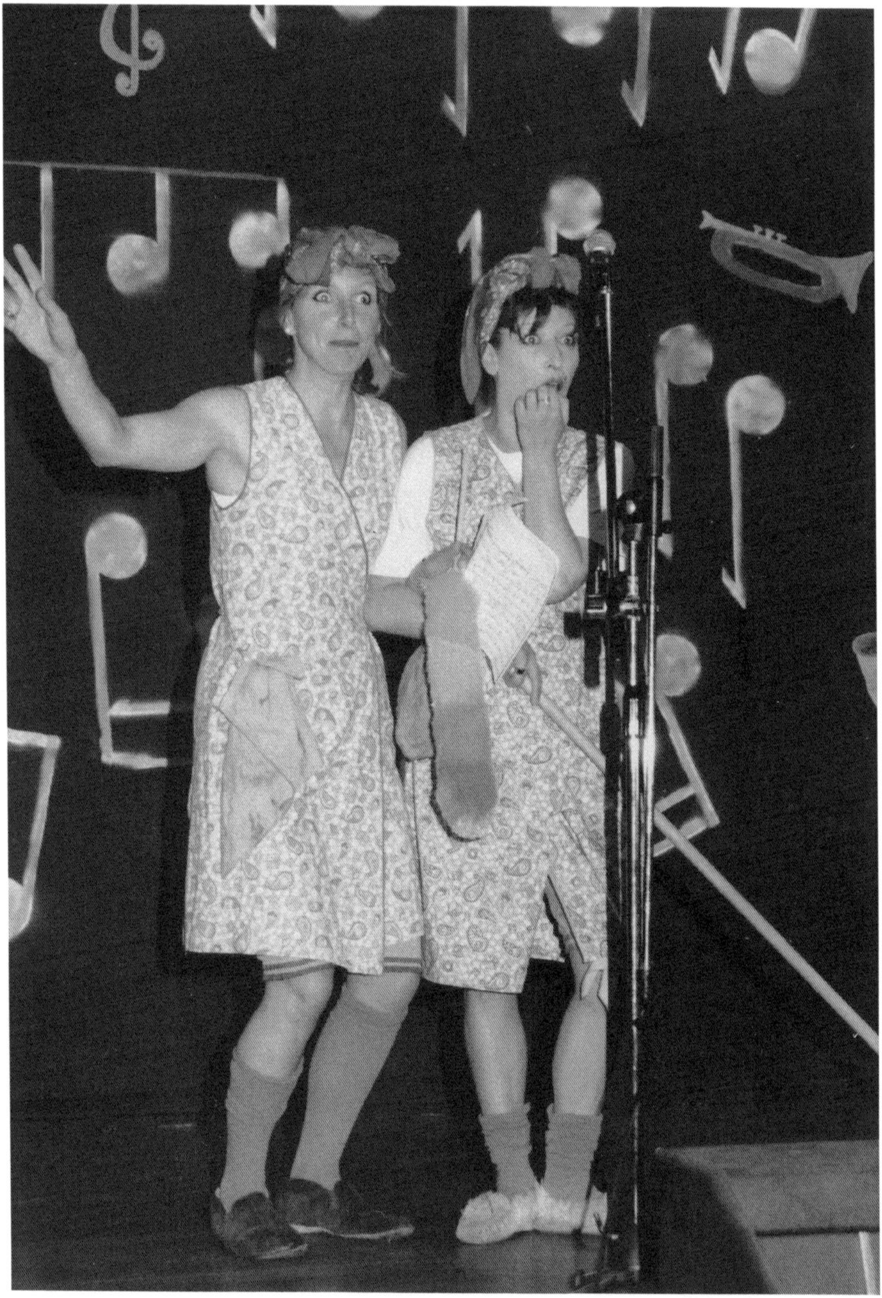

# Notes About the Poems

## A Chat with Sir John

**A Chat with Sir John**          **page 2**

In the late 1960's I was posted, as a police officer, to protection duties in Number 10 Downing Street when the poet, Sir John Betjeman, visited the building to show the Prime Minister's wife a painting he had acquired. It was an unscheduled visit and Sir John was asked to wait in the front hall while the staff contacted Mrs Wilson to inform her of the visitor. As he waited, he propped the portrait against the wall by the fireplace and chatted to me about the artist and the painting. What he said was interesting but I would rather he had talked about his poetry and Miss Joan Hunter Dunn. I waited for the chance to turn the conversation in that direction but in vain. All too soon Mrs Wilson was located and any opportunity disappeared when he was invited to attend the Prime Minister's private apartment.

**Where Purple Orchis Grew**          **page 3**

I listened to a tape recording, made in the 1970's, of Alice Martin. Alice had attended the village school and was a member of the congregation at Providence Chapel. She spoke about her childhood in the 1890's and how she and her friends used to roam the countryside around the village. She spoke so poetically that her words needed hardly any amendments or additions.

**The Fields Lie Silent Now**          **page 4**

I have walked the footpaths and fields around Charlwood for many years in all seasons. Probably always having a dog has provided me with the excuse for exploring the countryside I love. One early winter evening I was walking my old lurcher dog around Great High Field when a lone crow flew overhead and made for a group of oaks which were silhouetted against the setting sun. A song began to germinate. By the time my dog and I arrived home I had the backbone of the song and sang it to my wife. (She immediately tweaked the tune and gave it more substance.) The song could be about a rare slack period at the nearby airport but is actually a seasonal song about the fields at a peaceful time of day during a quiet time of the farming calendar.

127

### The 95th Came Home Today *page 6*

The little wooden building was the Guard Room of the barracks at Horsham where an experimental rifle corps was formed in the early years of the Napoleonic War. This corps became the 95th Regiment of the line. After the battle of Waterloo, the building was brought to Charlwood where it became Providence Chapel. In 2018 renovation work took place and the 95th's re-enactors society was invited to the grand re-opening. They attended in their green jackets with their rifles and fifes and drums.

### The Ghost of Betty Neighbour *page 7*

The traditional song about the Battle of Trafalgar captivated those present at the village sing-around in the old barn at the back of the pub. The dark winter night and the candle light seemed to add to the strange atmosphere created by the convincing words relayed by the singer. Years later I was told by an old village resident that in days gone by there existed an old hovel, at the edge of the orchard just a few yards from the barn, where an old lady called Betty Neighbour lived. He said that Betty always claimed that her father was one of the sailors who carried Lord Nelson below after he had been fatally wounded at Trafalgar. I thought that the ghost of old Betty Neighbour may well have contributed to the strange atmosphere at the village sing-around in the back of the pub all those years ago.

### They Sang the Barrel Dry *page 9*

One of the most regrettable aspects of modern farming is the passing of the old traditional harvest suppers on the local farms. A village lady told me of one of the last old-type harvest suppers which she had attended with her father at Tanyard's Farm, in Charlwood, in the 1930's.

### Missing from the Choir *page 10*

I spoke to the leader of our local ladies' choir and she told me of the sad occasion when the choir had to sing at the funeral, following the unexpected and premature death, of one of their very popular members.

### Gerald has Joined the Home Guard page 11

On the back of the old photograph of the self-conscious young man in military uniform Gerald Gillespie's mother had written, 'Gerald has joined the Home Guard. God help us.' Shortly after the photo was taken Gerald enlisted in the regular army and served until the end of the war. Gerald's son readily gave permission for me to expand on the theme and the poem was written.

### The Women in Red (AD 851) page 13

I remember being told at a very young age about 'the women in red' and how 'for many years water off the hillside flowed red.' The legend goes that after the Battle of Ockley in the year 851 the women of the village donned red garments and went out to meet and defeat a band of Danish warriors who were fleeing from the battlefield. Village place names such as Barebones, Rawbones, Slaughterwick and Killmans Bridge are said to be proof of the story's authenticity.

### Eighty Years Ago, Today page 16

An old man, born under the vapour-trailed skies of The Battle of Britain and who later survived the explosion from a German rocket, knows that since his precarious start in life every day has been a bonus.

### An Ancient Path in Modern Times page 17

One of my favourite walks in the village was from King's Whim into Highstile field and along Man's Brook passing Sawpit Field and Great Stevens Crawl but now the walk is interrupted by rows of landing lights and giant airliners, just above head height, as they take off or come in to land. Very occasionally, during a rare quiet time, the magic of the walk can still be recaptured.

### Darkness in the Evergreen page 19

Over half of the ancient yew tree in the churchyard had been damaged by fire; victim of an unknown arsonist. It was touch and go as to whether the tree, believed to be over a thousand years old, would survive. As it stood over the graves of their ancestors, the tree, being hollow, had for many generations provided a ready play-place for village children on their way to and from the church. The question asked was 'would the tree be there for future generations of village children as it had been there for their ancestors?'

### If the Stones Could only Speak
The village church, at the heart of the community, has seen the births, marriages, deaths and celebrations of the villagers for over nine centuries. When the Nicholas Room, the first addition to the building for over five centuries, was being built I stood and watched the stonemasons and builders as they worked, and thought 'If the stones could only speak?'

### The Echo of the Big Trombone
The old villagers told a tale of how the Rector, Parson Gibson, had sworn and shouted at the Village Band as they rehearsed on the Rectory lawn. He didn't like their music and threatened to throw their instruments in the Rectory pond. Over a century later, for several years, an all-day music festival was held in the churchyard close by the final resting place of the reverend gentleman who, as they say, 'must have been turning in his grave!'

### Keep in b' the Wall
After a night of old songs, stories and Irish whiskey spent around the big log fire, Jack's farewell call of 'Keep in b' the wall' would send us on our way as we walked out of his house into the cold early light of dawn.

### The Corner of the Field
As I've walked my dogs around the fields and woods the unspectacular view behind the corner of the field of the broken gatepost or the twisted tree trunk seems to have given me as much pleasure as the big vista of waving corn fields and sunsets over the hills.

### Don't go by way of the Old Church Walk
With its ancient yew trees and deep shadows between the gravestones many people are reluctant to walk through the Church Walk late at night. The prefer to take the longer route around Rectory Lane.

and the Second World War the church bells have been heard in the farms and fields around the village for eight centuries as they rang out their messages of births, deaths and marriages or called people together for worship.

### These Days my Doorbell Seldom Rings

Charlwood is a friendly community with an active church and many village clubs and societies but despite this there are still some residents who suffer from loneliness. I recall speaking to an old woman in the 1980's who proudly spoke about the achievements of her son who worked in a high-powered job and lived abroad with his wife and family. As she spoke, I gradually became aware that she somehow regretted her good intentions of not sending him to the village school and shielding him from other local influences which prevented him from becoming a village man.

### Tales that Skip and Dance over Time

Folk song and folk tales can be a gateway into the history of an area as they whet the appetite of the researcher to uncover the origins and unveil the facts behind the myth. Charlwood has its share of these old tales; some of them handed down through the centuries.

### The Fiddler's Shoe

When I lived in the old cottage opposite the Half Moon Inn my wife and I were alarmed one summer evening when splinters of wood started thudding against the leaded light windows. On going out into the street I found that a morris dancing team were performing the Upton upon Severn Stick Dance. Their enthusiasm and their clashing sticks caused splinters to scatter around the area in front of the parish pump. I recognised the old fiddler providing the music as the same fiddler I had seen many years ago, in my youth, performing at the same location.

### Wake up Boys and Follow Tom

Old Arky Standing often spoke about 'the men who followed the thresher' and how they used to liven up the village sing-arounds in the Half Moon tap room. He was talking about the farm labourers who had been made redundant by the arrival of the threshing machine and the traction engine. In the hope of finding a day's employment they would follow the traction engine from farm to farm. Tom Knapp, whose family were believed to have been resident in the village since Saxon times, was the driver and owner of the traction engine and was contracted by the farms around the parish to carry out the various tasks of each season.

### That Summer on The Somme
As a young 16-year-old Bumpy Illman survived the Battle of the Somme. Being badly injured on the first day he spent a period of recovery behind the lines. On his return to the front he found that his whole regiment had been posted as dead or missing. With the shadows of the horrors of war permanently lurking in his mind Bumpy, like many of his fellow survivors, could never bring himself to talk about his war-time experiences in later life.

### The Dawn Chorus
Along with the sun the dawn chorus circles the globe. At the first hint of sun-rise the birds start to sing. Will the permanent glare of increasing light pollution from an ever-expanding urbanisation eventually confuse the members of the choir and put an end to this beautiful feature of nature?

### That Wonderful Summer
Artist Alan King painted scenes of nostalgia. All his paintings evoked memories of my boyhood. I believe Alan included this poem in his sales literature to promote one of his exhibitions.

### The Last Hunt
Bill Pattenden of Spicer's Farm was the last survivor of those who had hunted with the ancient Charlwood pack of Old Southern Hounds. When speaking to Hugh Scott-Willey, just before the Second World War, he recalled how, as a young man, he hunted with the pack in the countryside around the village. Bill explained that the pack, believed to date back to Saxon times, had throughout its long life hunted only the hare and only on foot. The men often carried leaping poles to help them negotiate the deep ditches, streams and steep ghylls in the area. On hunting day mornings, the hounds would be summoned

from their various homes around the village by the huntsman blowing his horn. Bill remembered how, after eight centuries, the hunt was suddenly disbanded in the 1860's never to meet again. He recalled the last hunt.

### The Witch of Westcoat Wood                          page 57
A civil court case in the 1950's established that there was evidence of witchcraft having taken place in woodland just outside the parish boundary. A few years later, whilst walking my dog in the area, I happened to encounter and have a conversation with Cardel; the man deemed by the court to be a witch. I survived any spell he may have cast.

### When Biggie arrived at the Wicket                          page 61
As a boy I remember hearing the story of how, during his innings, Biggie Ellis had hit a mighty six and bounced the ball onto the steps of the Rising Sun pub over a hundred yards away.

### Now the Singing Days are Few                          page 63
In between songs Arky Standing would lament how the 'singing days are few' compared with the days of his youth. He would name a singer from previous days and talk about a particular song. He would then sing the song before naming another singer and repeating the process. After a whole evening reminiscing and singing 'the old songs' he'd say, 'Yes. It's not the same, now the singing days are few.'

### Old Soldiers of the Line                          page 64
It was a cold, misty morning and it was to be the last time that the First World War veterans were to march away from The Cenotaph after the annual Remembrance Day service. All traffic had been stopped in Parliament Square and the surrounding roads and I was standing alone in the autumnal murk of Great George Street. I was engulfed in complete silence and could hear nothing of the event that was taking place around the corner. There was no movement anywhere until suddenly I heard the sound of marching feet and a group of old men emerged from the November mist. They marched in perfect time and as they drew near a rich, melodic voice sang the first line of the song 'It's a long way to Tipperary'. His voice echoed around the tall government buildings on both sides of the street as his

marching comrades joined in. The song and the sound of tramping feet faded away as they disappeared into the gloom of St James Park and into the mists of history, never to march again.

### Clarkie's Ditch page 65

My wife, Susie, rushed into our cottage, opposite the Half Moon pub and demanded paper and pen. She told me that she had just been talking to one of the old village builders and had been told 'the best village story ever.' She wrote down the story of Clarkie's Ditch as told to her by the old man. The tale immediately took its place in our collection of village folk lore.

### The Lurcher Dog that Walked with Me page 67

We have rarely gone out specifically to acquire a dog; we have had some really lovely canine friends and most of them have somehow found us rather than us finding them. Cassie was a stray Lurcher dog who found herself on our door-step via procedures by dog wardens on both side of the county boundary. Dogs have been the motive behind me exploring the ancient ways and footpaths around, still beautiful, parts of Sussex and Surrey. It is hard for me to imagine life without a dog beside me.

### Go and Get Tula page 68

Tula was a Clumber Spaniel belonging to the actress Tallulah Bankhead who lived at the Manor House. When Miss Bankhead left the village to make a film in Hollywood, she left the dog with my grandfather. The actress never returned and Charlwood became Tula's permanent home. It was soon discovered that Tula had a talent for finding lost cricket balls in the hedgerows and undergrowth around the village cricket pitch. As soon as a batsman hit a six or a four into the bushes the cry of 'Go and get Tula!' would echo around the green. The cry could still be heard long after Tula died.

### Sweet Birdsong page 69

Despite the roar of jet engines overhead the wild birds still sing sweetly in defiant protest.

### Daniel's Challenge
page 77

At the end of the nineteenth century and into the twentieth Daniel Butcher was known as 'the strongest man in the parish'. He always accepted the chance to have a fight and could not resist a challenge. I remember hearing stories about Daniel in my boyhood and Arky Standing still entertained the locals in the village pubs with tales about 'ol' Dan'l' well into the 1960's.

### Much Squirming in the Pew
page 79

The concert, in the church, was to raise funds for the extension to the northern side of the building. The addition was to provide, after nine hundred years, a much-needed toilet for the congregation. The show was comprised of various scenes taken from the history of the village but a final song was needed. I thought a song about the need to 'spend a penny' over the centuries would be appropriate. The song had its opposition from those who thought it unsuitable for the location and amendments and alterations were suggested. In the end, by popular demand, the original version was sung.

### The Free Men of Charlwood
page 80

In their book of the same name, Ruth Sewill and Elisabeth Lane describe how the origin of the name of the village is derived from the Saxon Ceorls who populated the area. The Ceorls were freemen and the two authors suggest that their characteristics have been passed down the generations to create the independent nature of the village inhabitants throughout the ages.

### When Apted was in Hold
page 83

The villain Tom Apted was in custody and locked up safely in the village cage. The constable, Nicholas Blanchard, and his assistants repaired to the Half Moon for well earned refreshments. It was January 1792, the weather cold and wet but the Half Moon was warm and welcoming. The representatives of law and order were soon each enjoying a pint of local brew. They very soon enjoyed another and another. They enjoyed them for two whole days and nights and completely forgot about their prisoner in the cold and damp cage awaiting his court appearance.

For V.E. Day my mother had made me a red, white and blue suit and found a little Union Jack flag for me to wave. Dressed appropriately and waving the flag I stood alone at the end of the alley and waited for my father to return from the war. After about three hours I gave up and waved my flag indoors as I continued my vigil through the window. It was several long months before he arrived home bringing a bag full of souvenirs from foreign lands and the warm secure feeling of being a family once more.

Old George Prevett was one of the village characters of my boyhood. Renowned for his colourful language and his irreverent attitude there are many village tales concerning him. This is about his confrontation with an army doctor at Aldershot when he attempted to enlist at the start of the First World War.

The Gentlemen's Drinking Club met once a week in a public house just outside the parish boundary. On the surface the club appeared to be a well-run and orderly organisation with a Chairman, Secretary and Treasurer along with other designated officers, but in reality, the meetings were a cover for drunken and chaotic get-togethers. The only resemblance to a formal meeting was the keeping of minutes, but as these minutes could be added to by anyone at any time, they had little purpose or in fact little meaning. The minutes caused great amusement when read aloud at the start of the next meeting.

The school log-book for the 4th June 1915 states that the children were taken 'to the top of the lane in order to see the 5th Queen's Surrey Battalion of which Mr Farr (the Headmaster) is a member, march past.' Contrary to the poem Mr Farr survived the war and 45 years later was traced and taken out to dinner by his old pupils.

Yet another 'dog walking' poem about the countryside. On this occasion it was the countryside that nearly inspired me to write a song. I had the feeling that the song was there waiting to be written but drifted away before I could make any headway. The poem turned out to be about my inability to write the song.

### Waiting for the Ferry
I walked to the end of the jetty in Valldal, a small Norwegian village on the northern shore of Tafjord Fjord. The night was pitch black with no trace of any light pollution and a million stars shone in a clear sky and on the surface of the black water below me. I had stars all around me and seemed to be floating in space. Time stood still.

### Graffiti in the Blue
An article in the newspaper told of how youths had daubed a memorial to the airmen who had died in the Battle of Britain. I thought that those responsible were probably the same age as those whose names were listed on the stone.

### The Mariner's Tale
"Are you intending to go out on this tide?" said the man in the boat next to ours. "Because if you are, you have exactly four minutes!" We thought that he was joking and laughed but he wasn't and we didn't. He explained that we would be stranded on the Medway mud until the tide returned at midnight. We began to lose confidence in our captain when he showed surprise at the fact that the tides went in and out. We were fortunate that Rochester has so many good public houses.

### The Little Stove at Vardebu
The small mountain cabin was about four thousand feet above sea level. We didn't intend to stay but a sudden snow storm forced us to sojourn there for two days and two nights. The little iron stove in the corner and a pile of logs became the centre of our world for a while.

### The Day of the Numbers
In the early 1960's police officers in London were allocated a prefix to go with their warrant number and their divisional number. I combined this event with the apprehensions I had about 'the computer age', which was about to dawn, and wrote this view of the future, now slightly altered to include some modern terminology.

### When the Terror Time had Passed

Winston Churchill's wartime driver told me that, just after the end of the war, he was driving Mr Churchill back to London through Epping Forest when the wartime leader suddenly told him to stop the car. As the vehicle drew to a halt the Prime Minister alighted and walked off into the forest. It was a bright early summer day and the sun beams were filtering through the heavily laden branches onto a forest pool. All around the birds were singing. The chauffeur and protection officer caught up with the great man and found him quietly weeping under a giant beech tree. On enquiring as to why he was crying he said, "To think we nearly lost all this. Only I know just how close we really came!"

### Angle Tarn

Standing beside the little tarn in the Lake District I saw how quickly the clouds rolled down and banished the last rays of the winter sunshine.

### When Dublin Town Lay Sleeping

We could hear the sound of music being played on a tin whistle long before we actually saw the musician. The soaring notes echoed around the deserted night time streets of Dublin. It was the fiftieth anniversary of the 1916 Easter Rebellion and we had, by chance, that very morning met the survivors of the G.P.O. Garrison outside the building as they gathered to remember their comrades who had perished in the conflict. We eventually found the musician and walked along with him while he continued to play. We sang along as the music flowed but no conversation passed between us. After a tour of the town's back streets we arrived at a secretive and shadowy hall in a cobbled court yard. We were invited in and found the room to be filled with sinister-looking bearded men. Each man seemed to be clutching a musical instrument and beautiful music issued forth. We remained immersed in the music until the clear daylight of dawn showed through the chinks in the boarded-up windows.